D1195217

ALESSANDRA BURIGANA
MARIO CIAMPI

verbavolant

First published in 2006 by

Verba Volant Ltd.
Atlas House, Fourth Floor
1 King Street
London EC2V 8AU

© 2006 Verba Volant Ltd. London

Italian Designers at Home was created and produced by Verba Volant Ltd.

All rights reserved under International and Pan-American Conventions. No part of this book may be reproduced in any manner whatsoever without written permision from the publisher. Inquiries should be sent to Verba Volant Ltd.

verbavolant
e-mail: info@verbavolantbooks.com
website: www.verbavolantbooks.com

ISBN: 1-905216-03-3

Text: Alessandra Burigana
Translation from the Italian: Antony Shugaar

Printed in China by Sing Cheong Printing Co. Ltd.

Page 2: In the kitchen, the spare furnishings, including a large wooden table and American aluminum chairs, are embellished by the Achernar lamp, made of Murano glass, by Alessandro Mendini for Venini, 1993. (home of Alessandro Mendini)

Page 6: In the living room, a luminous panel with the figure of a horse, Anna Gili, 2001. The armchair, Richard III, was designed by Philippe Starck for Baleri in 1985. The red glass vase is from Anna Gili's Profili (Profiles) series designed for Salviati, 1997. (Casa Anna Gili)

Page 240: The Mobile Giallo (Yellow Dresser) chest of drawers, made of lacquered wood, is part of the Bharata collection by Ettore Sottsass for Design Gallery, Milano. It has a wooden base; the shelves are lacquered black. The knobs are covered with gold leaf. (home of Stefano Giovannoni)

Contents

Introduction

They have designed a great many objects for daily use—chairs, lamps, cutlery, armchairs, tables, household appliances, beds, and kitchen stoves—objects that have entered the everyday world of our domestic universe and our lives. They are the great industrial designers who have turned Italian style into a unique, world-renowned phenomenon. "The fact that in Italy, in the fifties and sixties, this phenomenon developed at the request of the manufacturers was a crucial factor," explains Vico Magistretti. "Italian design developed out of a very close relationship between industrial designers and manufacturers. That is why Italian design was more successful than the design that emerged from other countries: because of this intense and fertile dialogue between companies and designers."

We went to visit the designers, the masterminds of the success of Italian design, in their homes in order to understand the meaning that space has to those who design space for a living. We went to ask them to tell us how they live and whether they use the objects and the furniture that they have designed for others. And we discovered that they, too, have obsessions, passions, habits, dislikes, and little domestic rituals all their own. Who would have guessed that Enzo Mari is obsessed with miniature trees? Or that Michele De Lucchi is especially gratified by hand-carving wood to make little cottages and houses? That Ettore Sottsass is unwilling ever to throw away anything, out of a fear of definitive choices? That Fabio Novembre considers his house to be a metaphor for the Garden of Eden? Or that Vico Magistretti has a wardrobe custom-built to house his more than one hundred shirts, tailor-made in London? That Dino Gavina sleeps in a cube structure, in the center of his sixteenth-century living room, because he likes the cozy atmosphere of a sleeping car?

Every house has a unique story; every house is a surprise. "The stories of our lives are told by the little things," Sottsass told us. "What counts are the sensory aspects: the colors, the light, the sounds, the space, and the smells: these are all elements that we perceive with our senses." Furnishings, then, are not the only important elements in a house. In some cases, colors are all that are needed to create an environment, because inhabiting a home is a creative endeavor as well. There are those—like Massimo Scolari—who cannot live without books, and who have devoted a huge library room to reading. There are those who need lots and lots of space, and there are others who are satisfied with the panorama they can enjoy from their windows. There are those—like Mario Bellini—who love to surround themselves with artworks, and who even have their walls frescoed by a contemporary artist, and others who cannot stand to see even a single painting on the wall. Some, like Alessandro Mendini, seek out a situation of Zen-like emptiness; others "abhor a vacuum."

People often imagine that architects live in unusual, luxurious houses. That's not always the case. Some of the twenty-three industrial designers who opened the doors of their homes to us live in ordinary city apartments. A home—as they work to show us—is first and foremost a personal space where we should feel comfortable, in harmony with ourselves, without needing to prove anything to anyone. Perhaps that is why Riccardo Dalisi decided to have himself photographed—surrounded and overwhelmed by papers and prototypes—in his studio, which represents much more to him than a house: an apparently chaotic place, a place where, however, he manages to find inspiration and an internal equilibrium all his own. Some of them have decided to live in the country, in uncommon structures such as a former greenhouse or a sixteenth-century *barchessa* or a Venetian farmhouse. Others have found their ideal residence in a former industrial space on the outskirts of a large city. And there are those who have decided to live in a historic *palazzo* brimming with historic memories. What makes all these spaces special is not the size of the rooms or their spectacular decoration or their eccentric qualities, but rather that mix of culture, design, creativity, personal history, memories, interpretation, and exploration that makes each house unique and unrepeatable.

" *For me, it is necessary to live*
in relation to color, because I believe that
living is a creative act. "

Anna Gili was born in Orvieto, in Umbria. After taking her diploma at the I.S.I.A. (Istituto Superiore per le Industrie Artistiche, or Higher Institute for Artistic Industries) in Florence in 1984, she began to explore materials that created performances, such as the Abito Sonoro (Sonic Dress) at the PAC Padiglione d'Arte Contemporanea in Milan. She took part in the Milan Triennale, in 1985, with the Affinità Elettive (Elective Affinities). In the eighties, she worked with the Studio Alchimia and took part in exhibitions and events around the world. In 1989 she opened her own studio in Milan. She undertook design projects for Alessi, Salviati, Bisazza Mosaici, Metals, Play Line Swatch, Slamp, Cassina, Cappellini, TDK Japan, Dornbracht, and Ritzenhoff. She is an image director for many design companies. In 1992 she curated the exhibition Nuovo Bel Design at the Salone del Mobile, or furniture fair, in Milan. From 1996 to 1998 she was the art director and industrial designer for Pietro Rosa TBM, a manufacturer of scissors. She currently works with the Atelier Mendini for Nicolis Cola; she designs jewelry and produces a number of her own design objects under the trademark Anna Gili. She is the director of a design school in Verona, which forms part of the Accademia di Belle Arti, or Academy of Fine Arts.

Anna Gili recently moved into a loft in a reconverted industrial complex on the outskirts of Milan. It is an open space filled with symbols and signs that reveal her style. It is a space in which color predominates, with a very specific significance: "These colors are not chosen at random: the fuchsia, the dark blue, and the yellow are references to India: I love Asia, and my things reflect that sort of culture. I also love the contrast between these colors, so strong, against the absolute white of the walls. For me, it is necessary to live in relation to color because I believe that living is a creative act." Anna Gili began her professional career in 1984, with a performance tied up with body art, the *Abito Sonoro* (Sonic Dress), a theatrical and musical performance. "The idea was to go to New York and develop a career as an artist, because art has always been my vocation, while design has been a compromise, and it came about as a result. In Milan, the Studio Alchimia became interested in the *Abito Sonoro*, and it hosted my subsequent performances: the *Abito Monumentale* (the Monumental Dress), which was exhibited at the Triennale in 1985, *Le persone dipinte* (Painted Persons) in 1986, and *L'Abito a fiori* (Flowered Dress) in 1987." From

performances to installations, the evolution culminated in design: the *Tonda* (Round) armchair, one of her first design objects for the exhibition *Abitare il Tempo* in Verona, was manufactured by Cappellini.

The first thing one notices in the house is the kitchen, with cabinet doors made of colored glass, a clear reference to Mondrian. It is an open kitchen located, in an unusual fashion, in the middle of the house and establishing itself as the heart of the space. "According to *feng shui*, this is the area of the ancestors, and putting the kitchen here is appropriate. I like the fact that it creates a sense of centrality; cooking and looking out from within gives me a sense of freedom." The high-tech hood, suspended above the central counter, is oversized so that it can better capture the smells from cooking; the exhaust conduit that runs up from it resembles a giraffe's long neck. On the countertop of this technological yet New Age kitchen, are design objects and souvenirs of trips to the East, such as a Tibetan bell and a Buddha.

The three cats of the house, Biancone, Bianchetta, and Prince, leap acrobatically along the countertop, moving with agility and delicacy

among the fragile glass objects. "Once, they broke two really valuable pieces, but I can't put away everything. For that matter, they live in this house, too." The house radiates around a central patio: it was designed to capture as much light as possible on both stories. Next to the kitchen, separated by sliding walls, is the bedroom: "I decided to place it on the ground floor because I had the idea of differentiating the settings: the living area below, the studio above. I wanted to make sure that the upstairs had lots of light so that I could work there, while it's fine for the bedroom to have less light."

Heating such a large open space was a problem that was resolved with wall panels, making it possible to have a constant temperature at all elevations. Upstairs is the studio: along the cat-walk—which has a theatrical balustrade made of sheets of colored glass—a neon lamp punctuates one's progress. Each *Light Box* is decorated with a graphic symbol depicting an animal. In this technological space, the high-tech structure is enlivened by signs and symbols referring to the animal kingdom: the large luminous panels and the lamps form part of the *Arca di Noè* (Noah's Ark) collection, produced by Slamp, while the

chairs with stylized portraits of animals are produced by Anna Gili. In the bathroom, there is a segment of the *Mandàla con animali* (Mandala with Animals) created for the exhibition Essere e Benessere (Being and Well-Being) at the Milan Triennale, in 2000, linked to the Chinese zodiac, with symbols of the crocodile, the elephant, the deer, and the lion. "The structure is curiously modernist in style, but I am trying to create a pictorial effect with the colors. My research into the iconography of animals is the base of much of my design: they are psychological portraits, playful and colorful. These are my Umbrian roots that emerge: Renaissance portraiture had this particular aspect of the interior, psychological depiction. Progressively, I have increasingly distilled the images until they have become signs."

But are they design objects or art? "Design for me is something that has to do with art. Nowadays, in design, people talk about form and aesthetics, but the influence of status still plays a powerful role. By contrast, the Italian design of the fifties, the design of Castiglioni and Magistretti, had a poetics, a lyricism, an elegance that was not status."

Preceding pages, left: Anna Gili sitting on a chair with a stylized portrait of an animal. It forms part of the *SegnoDisegno* (SignDesign) collection, produced under the Anna Gili trademark. Behind her, a panel-lamp depicting a dog reissued by Anna Gili, 2001.
Preceding pages, right: In her studio, on a dresser, a one-of-a kind piece in lacquered wood made by Colombo Stile, 1985, stands a collection of small objects, souvenirs of her travels in Asia, and a scale model of the *Poltrona Proust* (Proust's Armchair) by Alessandro Mendini.

Above and opposite: The space, clearly of industrial origin, still has its original I-beams. The balustrade made of colored sheets of glass makes the space more fluid. In her studio, the *Elefante* (Elephant) panel-lamp forms part of the *Noah's Ark* series, by Slamp, 1999 (reissued by Anna Gili, 2001). The panel *Sheep* is in mosaic, by Trend, while the chair is an Anna Gili production. The table was designed by Alessandro Mendini. The neon lamps from the *Light Box* collection, depicting the signs of the Chinese zodiac, were produced for Anna Gili by ZAV.

Opposite: Upstairs, the *Poltrona Proust* (Proust's Armchair) by Alessandro Mendini, a luminous panel depicting a dog, and a chair from the *SegnoDisegno* collection.

Right: The kitchen, by Valcucine, dominates the space with its cabinet doors made of colored glass. On the countertop, glass vases designed for Salviati and Bisazza. On the near corner of the counter stands her first design object, the *Cro* ceramic vase for Alessi, 1985. Standing among objects from the Anna G. housewares collection, designed by Alessandro Mendini for Alessi, is a statue of a Buddha, to which Anna attributes protective powers, and a Tibetan bell. The small tables in terra cotta and are produced under the "Anna Gili" trademark.

In this house, which has a very marked industrial derivation (you can still see the original I-beams), what was needed was a warm material for the flooring: I chose a very durable prefinished durmast wood (a variety of oak). "Every material has its own calling. Now I am working with neon because it fascinates me as a sign in space. But I like glass a lot, too. I really got to know glass while working with glassmakers in Venice." The vases made of Murano glass are very colorful, with sinuous lines; Anna Gili designed them for Salviati and Bisazza, and they fill the house in every corner. "My design has a lot in common with organic design rather than rational design," she says. "It has a lot to do with Japan; the Japanese are the masters of organic design."

Anna Gili is one of the few women working in Italian design: "The world of design is a world that corresponds for the most part to a group logic. A woman, especially a creative woman, always tends toward autonomy, for cultural reasons." Anna Gili works with major companies, such as Cappellini, Cassina, Alessi, Bisazza, Salviati, Glass, Interflex, and Flou. She has also designed fashion accessories: a collection of eye-glasses for Swatch, in 1994; jewelry for Nicolis Cola, in 2001; and crystal boxes for Swarovski in 2002. Now she has decided to produce under the trademark "Anna Gili" the objects that she designs: functional lamps and chairs, which cost very little, but with the added value of a sign that has a lot to do with art. "This sign is not trendy. It forms part of my research. Because for me, design is in any case a form of art."

Anna divides her time between this loft and a country house in Umbria, where she is from and where she likes to return. But she also spends lots of time in Verona, where she teaches at the school of design within the Academy of Fine Arts there. "I would like to communicate to young people a critical approach to design. And I would also like to transmit to them what has been lost to some degree, that is, the tradition of Italian design bound up as well with the playful Mediterranean spirit. I think that it is not possible to do good design by copying other styles. I think what you have to do is find your way within your own culture."

Above, left: The three chairs, with backrests that have stylized portraits of animals, are from the *SegnoDisegno* collection, produced under the Anna Gili trademark. The table is *Parabel* by Eero Aarnio, produced by Adelta, 2002. In the corner is the *Scimmia* (Monkey) lamp and the long table on the left is *Karina* by Alessandro Mendini for Baleri, 1995.
Opposite: On the countertop, the *Rigati* (Striped) vases from the *Salviati* collection. The stove features an unusual hood with a long exhaust tube. The oven is from Bosch and the stove is from Smeg, Renzo Piano Design.

My research into the iconography of animals is the base of much of my design: they are psychological portraits, playful and colorful.

Above: In the living area is a luminous panel depicting a horse, Slamp, 1999 (reissued by Anna Gili, 2001). The *Tonda* (Round) armchair and an ottoman were designed by Anna Gili and manufactured by Cappellini, in 1991. The armchair on the right is by Philippe Starck for Baleri.

Opposite: The bedroom is visible on the other side of the patio. On the bed is a teddy bear designed for Ritzenhoff in 2000, and over the bed hangs a tapestry by Alessandro Mendini. Next to the tapestry is the entrance to the bathroom, featuring a section of the mosaic *Mandala with Animals*, designed for the exhibition Essere Ben Essere at the Milan Triennale.

" This is the house of the adult age. It is a comfortable house where image counts for very little and what really counts, instead, is the quality of life. "

Architect and industrial designer, Aldo Cibic was born in Schio, near Vicenza, in 1955. In 1979 he moved to Milan to work in the studio of Ettore Sottsass. The following year, the studio Sottsass Associati was founded. Also in 1980, under the leadership of Ettore Sottsass, the furniture collection Memphis was created, with Cibic as one of the designers and founders. In 1989 he began a career as a designer and entrepreneur with his own trade-mark, Standard. For Standard, he designed collections of very simple and functional furniture and objects. Since 1999 he has been designing the collection of ceramic and glass tableware for Paola C. where he is also the art director. With his own studio, Cibic & Partners (founded in 1989), he works actively in the fields of industrial design, interior decoration, and architecture. Among his most recent projects are: Medusa Multiplex movie theaters, 1999–2004; the headquarters of Abitare, Segesta, in 2003; the Selfridges department stores, Manchester, 2004; the offices of Dalla Verde, Vicenza, 2004. Among his recent exhibitions are: New Stories New Design, 2002, Citizen/City, 2003, and Microrealities, presented at the Biennale of Architecture in Venice in 2004.

Aldo Cibic has chosen to live in a villa up in the hills in the countryside around Vicenza, sur-rounded by an Italian-style garden with topiary hedges, stone statues, and even a belvedere, from which one can gaze out and enjoy the view of the countryside. For Aldo Cibic—with his American wife, Cynthia, and their son, Ian, six—this house represents the correct solution in this phase of his life. "I lived for many years in a loft, in Milan, and I really missed nature. I like the city too, but I am constantly traveling for work and when I come back home I feel as if I am on holiday."

In 1979 Aldo Cibic—at the youthful age of twenty-four—joined the studio of Ettore Sottsass, and together with Marco Zanini, Matteo Thun, Michele De Lucchi, George Sowden, and other young industrial designers founded Sottsass Associati. This marked the beginning of the thrilling adventure of Memphis: a mythical col-lection of avant-garde objects and furniture. In those years, Memphis did not represent merely a provocation thrown in the face of the rationalism of industrial design: it was a different design cul-ture. It was a phenomenon that ran against the current and that revolutionized the concept of

furnishing. The items designed for the collection emphasized geometric, eclectic forms, with bright colors and hyper-decoration. "For me, arriving as I did from the provinces, it was a radi-cal change in my life. I found myself at the center of a phenomenon of enormous creative energy, where everything was opened up for discussion, where form came before function. Working with Sottsass was a great opportunity."

In this large and light-filled house, the space is punctuated by the presence of furniture that is never banal, and always functional. "The chal-lenge was to 'domesticate' this house, to derive from a space—which originally had a radically dif-ferent purpose—a series of livable environments. This is the house of the adult age. It is a comfort-able house where image counts for very little and what really counts, instead, is the quality of life."

An unusual space, articulated into distinct but communicating environments. On the ground floor, the entry hall is filled with light— even on rainy days—thanks to a wall made entirely of glass. It used to be a greenhouse used to cultivate orchids. Today it reveals the passions of the owners of the house: natural materials, col-ors, lots of souvenirs from trips, photographs, art,

a few "historic" items designed by Aldo. "I always designed for myself, never to gain the approval of others, and I was never interested in becoming a name designer. In this house I made a special effort to understand how to make things that were 'un-designed,' to design something that would seem to have always been part of the house—such as the wardrobe in the studio, which is neither modern nor antique, but which looks like it has always been there. My dream was that this would not be a country house, that it would not be a designed house, but that it would be an unpredictable house, more poetic than designed. My design is not guided by an obsession with being contemporary, rather I have a need to follow my instincts."

In the center of the big hall is a table-soccer game, which he plays with his son. The protagonists of the space are animals, real and imaginary. A zoo of wooden, plush, plastic, and ceramic animals coexist serenely with the pets of the house— the dog, Lolo, and two cats—who play on the handsome Moroccan carpets. "There is constantly a hint of irony and a love of play; in this my wife helped me a great deal. If I lived by myself I would be much more of a perfectionist; instead, she

has a good practical sense, she keeps dogs and cats, she has to keep things in order, so it is all less formal and lighter, sunnier. This sense of the everyday is part of the house and it helps me to de-mythologize all the emphatic quality of the design."

The studio is separated from the entryway only by a glass wall. Everyone works at a single large table, Cibic's assistants and his wife; sometimes even his son does his homework there. This need to share spaces also emerges in the large kitchen, which is a sociable place. "This kitchen cost me a fortune!" Cibic says ironically. "Actually, I don't like glassy, perfect, technological kitchens, so I designed some simple furniture as containers, some very straightforward counters, and I had an artisan make them."

In the dining room, around the large wooden table that came from the Harry's Bar in Venice, there are several old folding movie-house chairs, purchased at an antiques flea market in Vicenza. They stand ready for guests who might stop by for lunch or to watch a movie. One corner of the living room can be turned into a little screening room; a white wall serves as the screen where they project all sorts of movies.

Preceding pages, left: Aldo Cibic photographed next to two unusual wooden bottle-shaped containers that he purchased in Morocco, placed as a pair of sentinels at the entrance to the living room, which was originally a stable.

Preceding pages, right: In the living area, the colorful low table near the window and the purple armchairs were designed by Cibic for Fratelli Boffi, 1997. Cibic also designed the *Porcino* (Piggy) stools, for Serralunga, 2004, and the hexagonal copper café table and the couch, both for Standard, 1991.

Above, left: The dog, Lolo lies on a striped carpe from Essaouira, purchased in Morocco, and next to an elephant made of chicken wire, the creation of Benedetta Mori Ubaldini.

Above, right: The large glass wall of the former orchid greenhouse, with sun-shade awnings. At the far end, a glass door separates the entrance area from Cibic's personal studio. At the center of the room, a table-soccer game, a Christmas present for his son, Ian.

Opposite: A view of the lovely Italian-style garden that surrounds the house. The bench is covered with mosaic tiles and was designed by Cibic for Bisazza.

" In this house I made a special effort to understand how to make things that were 'un-designed,' to design something that would seem to have always been part of the house. "

Right: The greenhouse as seen from the studio. The *Mia* chaise longue was designed by Cibic and manufactured by Paola C. in 2005; the lamp with the giant shade is called *Cynthia*, in homage to Cibic's wife, and it dates from 1993. The table and chairs are by Aldo Cibic for Standard, 1991.

Overleaf, left: An evocative nighttime view of the home from the garden. Above the former greenhouse, illuminated from within, there is a terrace with a balustrade that has stone statues and vases.
Overleaf, right: Towering in the entry hall is an enormous bear—wrapped in black adhesive tape—created by Cibic's nephew, Matteo Cibic. The bear was on display at MiArt in Milan and now lives next to a papier-mâché tiger from Sri Lanka.

What has become of the excesses, the hedonism of the eighties, the provocations of Memphis? Cibic was the first to leave the Sottsass Associati in 1989, setting up his own business producing his own objects under the label Standard. "I was really fed up with forms. I felt a need to design objects that were less the stars of the show, a little more approachable and friendly, for the pleasure of using them: chairs, dishes, tables that people would be glad to use." He says that his ideal aesthetic lies somewhere between man and those small things that can give us pleasure, even if only for a second.

Cibic does his best to spend at least three days a week at his home studio. In order to do that, he had to give up his job as design director at Fabrica, the center for communications research for Benetton. His work commitments take him, for the rest of the week, to Milan, where Cibic & Partners has its studio, as well as on trips around the world. Lately, he has been spending a great deal of time in China, where he has been working on a large factory outside Shanghai and with the University of Shanghai on a project that involves one hundred metro stations in outlying areas of the city.

Today, Cibic is increasingly uninvolved in production. At the center of his design exploration is man's relationship with the everyday world. More than design for production, Cibic is interested in the "design of services," that is, how spaces used by communities work. He has in mind a "city of vegetable gardens," where it would be possible for everyone to rediscover a relationship with nature. His *Microrealities* projects offer new poles of attraction, exchange, and service for the community. "It is not a romantic utopia; life is a project just like everything that forms part of it. There is a desire for less banal ways of living. Our actions define space and our inventions are a way of making new services that are lacking, services that everyone can use."

Above Cibic's home is an old lemon house surmounted by a tower. Cibic intends to set up a studio there and create spaces for young interns—one of his architectural utopias, on a reduced scale. In the end, it is an attempt to live everyday life in a better way.

Above: A view of the bedroom with a wall of bookcases in a light fir wood. The bed, or "bed sofa, and not a sofabed," according to Cibic, was built to plans by the master of the house. Next to the bed is a bathtub.

Opposite: The large kitchen is simple and cheerful. All of the furniture, except for the table and chairs, was designed by Aldo Cibic. Set on the hearth of the fireplace are bottles of wine, fruitstands, and other objects of everyday use. Everything has been designed with a eye toward simplicity; the utensils and cookware are in full view, and within reach. The big sink, reminiscent of those found in old Italian country houses, is made of pink marble. The table is set with ceramic tableware designed by Cibic for Paola C.

“ *Inhabiting a house means 'making your nest' and our general disposition is to make a home, but that is true whether it is the house where we live or a hotel where we stay during our many trips. We like to recreate a domestic situation that is not impersonal.* ”

ANDREA BRANZI

Andrea Branzi was born in Florence in 1938. An architect and industrial designer, he was a protagonist of the Radical Design movement and, from 1964 until 1974, a member of the group Archizoom. His work was included in the exhibition Italy: The New Domestic Landscape at the Museum of Modern Art in New York in 1972. In 1982 he founded the Domus Academy in Milan, a postgraduate design school. From 1983 to 1987 he was the editor of the magazine Modo and he has also contributed to such magazines as Domus, Interni, and Casabella. He is considered to be one of the leading figures in neo-modern design. Among the many books Branzi has written are La casa calda: Esperienze nel nuovo design italiano (1984), Animali domestici (1987), and Pomeriggi alla nuova industria (1988). He has had solo exhibitions at the Triennale di Milano and in galleries and museums around the world, including the Musée des Arts Décoratifs at the Louvre in Paris, the CAYC in Buenos Aires, and the Lijbanam Centrum in Rotterdam. He won the Golden Compass in 1987 for his body of work. Branzi has worked for Alessi, Cassina, Vitra, Zanotta, Artemide, Interflex, Up & Up, Lapis, Acerbis, Design Gallery Milano, Dornbracht, and Vorwerk. Currently Branzi teaches design at the Politecnico di Architettura in Milan.

Andrea Branzi and his wife, Nicoletta, made an unconventional choice. A few years ago, they left the center of Milan and their home in Brera—the fashionable neighborhood of artists—and moved to Bovisa, an industrial area that is becoming a university campus. The Bovisa section of Milan was filled with factories, but in recent years it has undergone a transformation. The university facilities that have moved to the northern section of Milan—the Politecnico, or Polytechnic University of Milan, to Bovisa and the *Statale* (or State University) to nearby Bicocca—have led a process of Milanese urban renewal.

The architect Branzi renovated a former artisanal workshop in Dergano, near Bovisa, dating from 1932. "We wanted to have our studio and our home close together, for the sake of convenience. I teach at the Department of Design the Politecnico and I do design research, based on models that we produce ourselves, so I also need a space for the workshop where we make our prototypes. Design research is a rather special sector of the profession as it is practiced today. It is independent and not closely tied to the manufacturer: this type of professional organization with only a few employees has allowed me

to put together 'home and workshop'" says Andrea Branzi.

The Bovisa campus of the Politecnico is in the vanguard in terms of infrastructure and workshops, one of the leading areas in all Europe. The Brera Academy of Fine Arts is about to move here, and plans are being developed for a space that will house facilities for research, exhibitions, events, and conferences—all centered on the theme of design.

Branzi's studio is linked by an interior staircase to the residence, where there are prototypes of chairs and lamps that the architect is observing on a provisional basis, "but these are temporary presences. There aren't a lot of my own items here. I am not interested in collecting them. Otherwise, my home would become a showroom."

Andrea Branzi was a leading figure of what was known as "radical design" with the group Archizoom, which was, at the end of the sixties, a promoter of a new idea of industrial design, based upon experimentation and research. He took part in such avant-garde movements as Alchimia and Memphis; he was the editor of the magazine *Modo*, and in 1982 he founded Domus

Academy, a school for design that introduced its students to design as an avant-garde workshop.

"I studied in the city of Florence, a place where conditions were not particularly favorable for the modern approach, but my thesis project is now in the collection of the Centre Pompidou in Paris. I took my degree in 1966, in Florence, and times were tough. There were many people working against us. Struggling to impose your own ideas is part of the privilege of being a member of the avant-garde."

The residence is a home/workshop, a loft where the environments and their functions are not clearly defined. The kitchen and the living room form a single open space. A corridor running lengthwise links the bedrooms and the bathrooms. The light here is extraordinary because there are no houses across from the building: it is a luminous space thanks to the perimeter walls with expansive windows that render the interior practically transparent.

Design items and souvenirs from trips coexist, a mute testimonial to the passions of the master and mistress of the house for objects, both everyday objects and those that are anything but quotidian. "There is no overarching plan in our domestic stage setting: things arrive in our house, they are placed here or there for a while, and then they go away. Things are put together a bit at random," says Nicoletta. "The objects are provisional because it is nice for every period of life to have a profile of its own, an array of objects that accompany it. All things considered, when you accumulate too many things, you tend to mix together periods of your life that now belong to the past. You don't always have the courage to get rid of things. The great pleasure of coming to live in this house was that it gave us an opportunity to toss out an amazing mass of things!"

Furniture and objects have a perfect relationship with the space; the same is true of the large tables made of solid wood and the impalpable lamps made of "paper," which spread a diffuse light and seem to hover in the air. The form of light is one of the favorite subjects of Branzi's research. "Since a lamp changes identity when it is turned on and when it is turned off, it emanates different feelings. I like to use materials that are present in the Asian tradition, such as wood, bamboo, and paper, which is fragile, but fragility has a very positive value in Japanese culture."

Preceding pages, left: Andrea and Nicoletta Branzi with their dogs. They are seated in the living room on a prototype couch next to a *Newton* lamp for Omikron Design and a *Potto* magazine holder, no longer in production, designed by Andrea Branzi for Zanotta.

Preceding pages, right: On the shelves that run beneath the windows are three plastic tube models of vases from the *Blister 2004* collection, by Andrea Branzi for Design Gallery, Milano.

Above: In the living room, an image from the installation *Paper Garden 1* by Andrea Branzi for the Museo di Santa Maria della Scala in Siena is projected on the far wall. The standing lamp made of paper, bamboo, and marble is by Andrea Branzi, for Design Gallery, Milano.

Opposite: An ample sofa by Aldo Cibic for Standard, a prototype table, and *Lubekka* chairs designed by Branzi for Cassina. Above the bookcase on the left is a wall hanging embroidered by Nicoletta Branzi. Between the windows sits an antique cast-iron Chinese stove.

Overleaf, left: The bedroom. The flooring of the entire living space is composed of larch-wood recycled from freight cars. The loft has large industrial windows on two sides and beneath the windows of the bedroom is a series of tanganika wood containers with glass countertops, designed by the owners of the house. The light is ideal for the orchids that Nicoletta Branzi cultivates; she has quite a collection.
Overleaf, right: The kitchen space of Casa Branzi is defined by parallel counters. The frames are made of masonry, the countertop is Carrara marble, and the cabinet doors are made of bleached and varnished wood. The basket-lamp on the counter on the left was designed Branzi and produced by Argentaurum Gallery, Belgium. The hanging lamps were also designed by Branzi and were produced specifically for this home by Omikron Design.

Second overleaf: On the glass shelves in the living room, a series of geometric vases, models for the *Blister 2004* collection by Andrea Branzi for Design Gallery, Milano.

Around the table, a prototype, are *Lubekka* chairs, designed by Branzi for Cassina, the lamps designed for Design Gallery, Milano, and the *Newton* lamp for Omikron Design. At the center of the room is a sofa designed by Aldo Cibic for Standard of which the dogs of the house are the chief occupants.

This room is also the domain of Nicoletta, who has a special love for Asian cultures and who studied Japanese. Nicoletta creates beautiful wall hangings with embroidery threads. She shows us a strip of linen, three and a half yards long, on which she has embroidered a series of Japanese poems and ideograms: the symbols for family, strength, rest, dream, and peace. "I made it for one of my two daughters, for her to hang behind the headboard of her bed."

Between two windows is a Chinese cast-iron wood stove: beneath all the windows runs a series of tanganika wood containers, with a thick glass shelves on them, made to designs by the owners of the house. It is an optimal solution for keeping everything in order without cluttering up the central space with other containers.

Two parallel countertops define the workspace of the kitchen, which has a masonry structure, a countertop made of Carrara marble, and bleached and varnished wooden cabinet doors. The central lighting is provided by a line of lamps in opaline glass, hanging from a steel bar, custom made. They alternate with bunches of dried flowers that hang from the bar, as in a country house. In the bedroom, a few essential furnishings: at the head of the bed is a Tibetan tapestry purchased from Etno Arte, while the reading lamp is from Ikea.

"Inhabiting a house means 'making your nest' and our general disposition is to make a home, but that is true whether it is the house where we live or a hotel where we stay during our many trips. We like to re-create a domestic situation that is not impersonal." Hence the necessity to surround oneself with friendly presences, recognizable and familiar signs.

In this house, technology is present, but it is not noticeable. Branzi's design philosophy always includes technology on one side and aesthetic research on the other. Objects have a great importance in our everyday lives from a functional point of view, but also in symbolic, emotional, and psychological terms.

DENIS
SANTACHIARA

Denis Santachiara was born in Campagnola (Reggio Emilia) in 1951. He was self-taught as an artist, and he began working as a designer in the car-body sector. In the seventies, he oversaw installations and exhibitions for museums. He took part in the Venice Biennale and the Milan Triennale. He designed computers for Italtel and cell phones and video recorders for Panasonic. He decided to devote himself entirely to industrial design, working with many Italian and international furniture manu-facturers: FontanaArte, Artemide, Naos, Campeggi, Desalto, Baleri. Today his research is focusing on his Personal Factory, a revolution in design that will allow anyone to create their own objects with a sort of three-dimensional Internet.

The apartment where Denis Santachiara lives is in a working-class neighborhood of the old part of Milan, right across from the Colonne di San Lorenzo, a line of ancient Roman columns. It is the objects that furnish it that make it special. As soon as you enter the living room, you are greeted by an oversized lamp with an exagger-ated lampshade. You soon discover that inside the lampshade is a full-fledged home office, with a computer, printer, and everything else you might need to work. This lamp—ironically called *Angel*, because the two white wings of the lampshade open and close, like wings—was designed for Naos. The surprises aren't over. Incorporated into this piece of equipment is also a home theater, with everything you need to project movies on the facing wall. *Angel* contains all the key elements of Santachiara's design philosophy: "Because the effect of surprise forms part of a more general strategy: the new idea is not so much a matter of whether objects are beautiful or not, but really that they play jokes, or gags, and these gags become a new aesthetic territory."

In his apartment, there are many moving objects: a lamp that changes color with a remote control, designed for Artemide; armchairs that rock, designed for Baleri, folding chairs for Vitra. Santachiara enjoys using technology as a playful element with which to design objects that are multifunctional and that transform themselves. There is an ottoman that contains an inflatable mattress so that it becomes a bed; a lamp that becomes a table; a pillow that turns into a stool. "I always try to transform an object into some-thing else," says Santachiara with amusement. "I even wrote a little glossary of mine where the key words are: animation, fiction, interaction, trans-formability, performance, technology, and poetry. I believe that people nowadays are nomadic. The concept of the nomadic home underlies my transformable furniture: the ten-dency is to move often, and so objects should be more agile and versatile."

In his living room, he shows us an odd table, which remained at the prototype stage, with a transparent double top made of glass that also becomes a display case for pictures, photographs, pressed leaves: it takes its inspiration from those café tables from the fifties that had a sheet of glass over the tablecloth to keep it from getting stained.

But the most surprising thing is the wall behind the table. Santachiara has removed the shelves that formed a long bookcase running along the wall and has left only the support brackets: "This forces me to be more selective, because I can't keep everything, and especially I have to change things according to the trips I take, the people I meet, and so my home is constantly changing."

Santachiara has lived in this apartment for twelve years, but he has not accumulated anything. "I tend to empty out a space. I am constantly traveling. I own more suitcases than I do furniture, and I come back home at night to sleep." He says that he does not like overdesigned houses, used primarily for official entertaining, houses and apartments that are designed with public relations in mind: "A house is nice if it expresses your personality, even if it's a mess, even if it's unattractive." His apartment is concentrated in the living room and on the very large terrace, where he occasionally has his friends over for a party. Santachiara began his career working for an automobile coachbuilder. "I am pretty well self-taught and that was my first design school." For a while he worked as a painter: he would

paint hyperrealistic figures, treated as if they were a design project. Then he went on to do installations for exhibitions, galleries, and museums, which "were in any case already design projects": installations for the Milan Triennale in 1978 and for the Venice Biennale in 1982. Finally he became involved in industrial design, and he moved to Milan. "I understood that I was interested in working on a form of design that could also be a form of artistic expression, and so it was. The first object I designed for production was for FontanaArte; before that, I had only done one-offs for exhibitions."

Many years ago he designed his first animated objects for the *Modula* collection by Domodinamica: a doormat with a little songbird that would sing every time you stepped on it, a lamp with sheep that would go baa when you turned it on. "This corresponds to a broader philosophy: that objects are increasingly intelligent, interactive, and can now memorize, speak, and listen. All these immaterial, nonphysical elements—industrial design must manage them, endow them with an aesthetic, functional, communicative, emotional nature. And this is the aspect that is most typical of me."

Preceding pages, left: Denis Santachiara with his inevitable cigar, in front of the "equipped" wall in his living room.

Preceding pages, right: The lamp is one of those surprise objects that Santachiara invents, *Olympiona* for Domodinamica, 1986. When it is turned on, a cloth flame emerges and flutters, as if it were a torch.

Above, left: A corner of the living room with a view of the Colonne di San Lorenzo. The chair with a removable cushion that becomes a stool is by Santachiara, and the lamp, *Niobe*, which changes color with a remote control, is also a design by Santachiara, for Artemide.

Above, right: The appliqué lamp is a mask in transparent glass, a prototype designed by Santachiara.

Opposite: Santachiara has placed objects on shelf brackets: rubber shoes worn by Japanese cleaning ladies, an old painting of his, an aboriginal drawing he found in Australia. The table is a prototype. It has a double glass surface that serves as a vitrine for photographs, pressed leaves, and drawings: an evolving picture frame. The chair made of resin in a natural mustard color is by Verner Panton, from the sixties. The two chairs behind the table are examples of the *Santa Chair*, Vitra, 1998.

Opposite: The luminous living room is almost empty: a rocking armchair designed for Baleri, an Algerian carpet from the nineteenth century, a few iron cabinets and the *Pisolò* ottoman that conceals an inflatable mattress, produced by Campeggi.
Above, left: A collection of objects that wobble and predict earthquakes, *I tre moschettieri*, designed by Santachiara for the Japanese company Marutomy.
Above, right: The oversized *Angel* lamp designed for Naos, 2002, conceals within the giant shade a complete home office and a home theater. The lamp *Olympiona* that, when it is turned on, emits a fluttering fabric flame.

He offers the example of the personal computer, a machine that is used for work but also for entertainment purposes, for things involving feelings. "In the eighties, I designed computers for Italtel. I designed video recorders, cell phones for Panasonic: I tried to renew the old rituals with new technologies. I wanted to make a movie camera that you could turn off by blowing on it as if it were a candle."

In a corner of the living room, there are metal cabinets that he found in a technical shop, made with an unusual galvanized finish: metal is his favorite material, and he likes soft materials for contrast. For the most recent Salone del Mobile, or furniture fair, in Milan, he designed a pillow that massages your back, for Campeggi; a luminous lamp that also works as a fan, for FontanaArte; a living room café table that becomes a cart, a lamp that becomes a table, a clothes hanger that makes garments disappear for Naos; a stool that rises and descends for Domodinamica, and, for Desalto, a box that opens and becomes a large bookcase. Santachiara has a mania for giving his objects odd names: *Babà*, *Pisolò*, *Sciuscià*, *Cu-letto* (for a cushion bed). The idea is to design objects that are also

subjects, and in the end, even the name you choose helps to humanize objects.

Now Santachiara is doing exploratory research on the industrial design of the future. A genuine revolution in the area of industrial design is embodied by his *Personal Factory* that will let anyone produce their own objects in a rapid and automatic way. "I am working on the *Personal Factory*, a sort of three-dimensional Internet that will allow anyone to build objects via the Web. There is no warehouse, no production, no distribution, all you do is download a technical design onto a server and you have it made. The only limitation is that the materials are still relatively few in number and the costs are still quite high, but many small objects can be made via the Internet. This is a new frontier that fascinates me. The role of the industrial designer is no longer to design specific objects, but rather to design strategies, an area that is conceptual and entirely virtual." He admits that he enjoys his work as an industrial designer: "I have always felt as if I were playing instead of working, with the excitement of gambling." And he takes a deep and evidently pleased puff on his cigar, and the smoke becomes part of his home.

" On the walls, there wasn't room for many paintings, and so I decided that the doors would be perfect as artworks. "

CLETO
MUNARI

Cleto Munari began his career in the world of industrial design following his acquaintance and friendship with Carlo Scarpa, from 1972 until 1978. From 1980 until 1984, he was a business partner with Ettore Sottsass. In 1983 he founded the Cleto Munari Design Associati, headquartered in Vicenza, and the Cleto Munari Asia, headquartered in Hong Kong. With the production of his design creations (1978–82) he also held his first cultural events, sponsored by city governments and the departments of architecture at the universities of Venice and Naples. Objects produced by Cleto Munari Design are in the collections of over one hundred museums around the world, including the Museum of Modern Art of San Francisco, the Denver Art Museum, the Metropolitan Museum, and the Museum of Modern Art in New York. Among his most important exhibitions are: Belvedere Osterreichische Galerie (Vienna, 1986), Presidential Castle of Prague (Prague, 1993), Centre Pompidou (Paris, 1989), Kunstmuseum (Düsseldorf, 1983), the National Museum of Modern Art (Jerusalem, 1985), Seibu Museum (Tokyo, 1988), and Deste Gallery (Athens, 2003). The most notable exhibitions in Italy were at the Castel Sant'Angelo (Rome, 2000), Palazzo Medici (Florence, 1987), Palazzo Reale (Naples, 1997), Ca' Masieri (Venice,

Cleto Munari has achieved a great many of his dreams. One of those dreams was to produce contemporary design objects, created by the greatest architects of the world. He succeeded—in over thirty years of business—with the collaboration of 150 world-famous designers, such as Carlo Scarpa, Ettore Sottsass, Alessandro Mendini, Arata Isozaki, Michael Graves, Vico Magistretti, Gio Ponti, Alvar Aalto, Tapio Wirkkala, Gae Aulenti, and Michele De Lucchi. A designer himself, but also a patron of the arts, he has produced some twelve thousand objects, including a unique collection of architectural jewelry (an homage to his wife, Valentina); a collection of watches; a collection of extraordinary pens, designed by five Nobel laureates; a prestigious collection of one hundred chalices made of Murano glass, and numerous objects made of silver, which form part of the permanent collections of over one hundred museums around the world. "I hadn't planned to create a manufactory; rather, I was thinking about an 'art atelier' that might create truly unique objects."

Another dream was to renovate a sixteenth-century villa, in Brendola, just outside Vicenza—to restore it to its original magnificence with the

assistance of a contemporary architect, Hans Hollein. And then go to live in it. According to the maps of the old tax rolls, the villa originally had a military lookout tower. The tower was demolished when the villa became a private home. Hollein's idea was build a transparent glass tower—a reference to the past—that would offer a breathtaking view of the Berici Hills.

But the entire country complex was under the protection of the *Beni Ambientali*, or Department of Environmental Resources. "It was a utopian endeavor to undertake such an innovative renovation," Cleto Munari explains. "The *Soprintendenza* rejected four different designs and Hollein, after a thousand bureaucratic stumbling blocks, resigned from the project. I really believed in the idea of a contemporary architectural sign implanted into an ancient context. At that point, I surrendered and decided to leave the villa just as it had been, a noble and evocative relic."

Until then, Munari had lived in a Palladian *palazzo* in the heart of Vicenza: the family home, sumptuous but inconvenient. He shifted his focus to a building adjoining the home, once used by peasants, which had a difficult shape to work

43

1983), and the Basilica Palladiana (Vicenza, 1993). In addition to working with silver and glass in his own manufacturing facilities in Padua and Murano, Cleto Munari has worked with world-renowned architects on diverse projects in urban furnishings (lighting for the airport of Fiumicino, Rome), interior design (Catullo airport in Verona), and the production of gold jewelry, watches, and fountain pens.

with: it was six meters by fifty meters (twenty by one hundred sixty-five feet). On the ground floor, it had been broken up into five residences, with five chimneys, while on the upper story there was a huge grain silo. Cleto Munari needed to create a functional space that might house a portion of his collections and tell the story of his great loves: contemporary design and informal art.

He redesigned the space of the daytime living area, demolishing some walls to create a number of rooms leading one into the next. "The nice thing about this house is the fluidity and the circularity of the space: at each end of the house there are two different staircases that connect with the nighttime living area, allowing a certain degree of independent movement."

On the ground floor, there is a living space, with various parlors, the studio, and the kitchens. Upstairs, there are bedrooms with their bathrooms. According to Munari, freedom is a fundamental element of living well. This is the reason that he designed not one but two kitchens. One of these kitchens is used exclusively by his wife, Valentina, who is Neapolitan and, in keeping with a certain Neapolitan tradition, likes to cook without anyone bothering her. In this setting,

Munari designed three blocks of furniture that are complementary but quite distinct; these pieces of furniture are a clear homage—in both color and shape—to Mondrian. The blue, the red, and the yellow mark the various functions: water (sinks and dishwashers), fire (ovens and ranges), and cold (refrigerators and freezers). They were manufactured by Valcucine, with Rex Built-In appliances. Adjacent to this colorful kitchen, there is another entirely white kitchen, very rigorous in style. It is used by the staff of the residence.

In order to make this home special, Munari carried out a unique decorative project on the three-meter-tall (ten-foot) doors. "On the walls, there wasn't room for many paintings, so I decided that the doors would be perfect as artworks. I asked my friends, both architects and designers, to create an unmistakable sign on the doors: Mimmo Paladino, Milton Glaser, Alessandro Mendini, and Ettore Sottsass, all enthusiastically agreed to send me sketches, which I then saw to putting into production." The items of contemporary furniture were also the creations of architect friends, and they coexist harmoniously with the large eighteenth-century

Preceding pages, left: Cleto Munari is sitting on the *Poltrona Proust* (Proust's Armchair) by Alessandro Mendini, Alchimia, 1978 (reissued by Cappellini, 1993).
Preceding pages, right: A view of the barchessa that Munari renovated and transformed into a residence.

Left: The large mosaic panel that depicts a fish-serpent, by Alessandro Mendini.
Above: A corner of the living room, with a large seventeenth-century painting by Cesare Fracanzani.
Opposite: A view of the living room, which has a floor made of Greek marble, like the floor of the loft, which is visible in this photograph. The door at the far end of the room is by Milton Glaser; the paintings by Fracanzani and the eighteenth-century Neapolitan furniture are family heirlooms that belong to Munari's wife, Valentina.

44

Left: An odd console table made of colored boxes, a one-off designed by Ettore Sottsass for this house. Atop the console table, a centerpiece by Hans Hollein and the Tao Ho sculpture by Walter Gropius. The yellow door is by Mimmo Paladino, while the door at the far end is by Alessandro Mendini.
Above: A door designed by Alessandro Mendini.
Opposite: The Valentina kitchen, built by Valcucine, to plans by Cleto Munari. Three blocks of cabinets define the three zones of the kitchen. Three mask-lamps over each block are the warrior protectors of the kitchen. The chairs, *Ant*, are by Arne Jacobsen for Fritz Hansen.

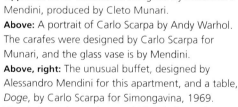

Opposite: Silver candelabra designed by Alessandro Mendini, produced by Cleto Munari.

Above: A portrait of Carlo Scarpa by Andy Warhol. The carafes were designed by Carlo Scarpa for Munari, and the glass vase is by Mendini.

Above, right: The unusual buffet, designed by Alessandro Mendini for this apartment, and a table, *Doge*, by Carlo Scarpa for Simongavina, 1969. The chairs, *Tulu*, are by Kazuhide Takahama for Simongavina.

Overleaf, left: On the shelves in the loft, a collection of glass items made for Electrolux. Starting from the left, on the lowest shelf: vases by Cleto Munari, Jacques Bedel, Melanie Weissweiler, Giovanna Portoghesi, Kurokama, Alessandro Mendini, and Flavio Albanese. On the middle shelf, all glass items are by Ettore Sottsass, except for the last one, by David Palterer. On the top shelf: glass items by Hans Hollein, Borek Sipek, Izzika Gaon, and Marco Zanini.

Overleaf, right: On the bottom shelf, glass items by Cleto Munari, Hollein, Zangrandi, Albanese, Mendini, Zucchi, and Richard Meier. Above them are vases by Ettore Sottsass and David Palterer.

French and Neapolitan mirrors, with the seventeenth-century Neapolitan furniture and oil paintings—by Cesare Fracanzani—which his wife, Valentina, a descendent of an aristocratic family from Naples, refused to give up.

But the constant and particular presence that can be detected in all the spaces of the house is that of Carlo Scarpa, a crucial figure in the private and professional life of Cleto Munari. "He was my teacher, my mentor, and my closest friend. I enjoyed watching him work, and if I am anyone today, I owe that to him. In design I am self-taught, but I had a good understanding of and familiarity with the materials, the techniques, and the workshops, and this helped me a great deal. My adventure in the world of design began with Carlo Scarpa; he used to say that I had a good sense of proportion. In 1977 I asked him to design a nice set of handsome, functional cutlery: he insisted that they be made of gold and silver. This was a demanding project, but it also marked a turning point in my career as an entrepreneur." The large dining room table, too, is by Carlo Scarpa, as are the silver carafes and the linear cornice (or mantelpiece) of the fireplace. Hanging over the buffet, in the dining room, there is also

a collage, *Omaggio a Carlo Scarpa*, by Andy Warhol. "I bought it after Scarpa died, in 1978. His widow didn't want it anymore, she didn't like the way that Warhol had depicted her late husband."

Everywhere, there are objects of art and design: chairs by Arne Jacobsen, a sculpture by Walter Gropius, blown-glass vases by Borek Sipek. On the stairs, which Munari wanted to be as transparent as possible, there are paintings by his friends: Francesco Pernice and Gaetano Pesce. In the hallway that leads to the guest bedrooms, there is a collection of vases and objects in glass, designed by Paolo Portoghesi, Izzika Gaon, Toni Cordero, Borek Sipek, and Munari himself. A home-qua-gallery? "Instead, I would call it an ideal space in which to tell my own story, where the modern objects are in harmony with the antique setting." What is the next dream he hopes to achieve? "The most important thing is always whatever I'm going to do tomorrow. Now I'd like to restore the ruins of the villa and establish a foundation or a museum of design, in order to collect, here in my land of birth, all the sketches, designs, and collections that I have produced."

" My ideal is that there should be very few things in my home. I would describe myself as an orderly person, with a tendency toward the casa povera. "

ALESSANDRO
MENDINI

Alessandro Mendini was born in Milan in 1931. After taking his degree in architecture at the Politecnico, or Polytechnic University of Milan, he began his work as a designer in the studio of Nizzoli Associati. He worked also in the field of journalism: he was the editor-in-chief of Casabella, *and in 1977 he founded the magazine* Modo. *He took over from Gio Ponti as the editor-in-chief of* Domus. *In the eighties, with the Alchimia group, he explored the theme of Radical Design. With Branzi and Sottsass he was a leading supporter and force behind the renewal of Italian design in those years. He received the Golden Compass award twice, in 1979 and in 1981. In 1989, he founded, with his brother Francesco, also an architect, the Atelier Mendini. Together they designed a tower in Hiroshima, Japan; the Fabbriche Alessi; the new Olympic swimming pool in Trieste; a number of stations of the Metropolitana and the restoration of the Villa Comunale in Naples; the Museum of Groningen in Holland; and buildings and shops in Europe and in the United States. With his design, he has reinvented the image of Alessi, and he has done design projects for Hermès, Zanotta, Swatch, Philips, Venini, Cartier, Glas, Cappellini, and Bisazza.*

The apartment where Alessandro Mendini lives, in Milan, is a space where work, experiences and experiments, and domestic life all flow together. The apartment is connected to the studio, the Atelier Mendini, by a steep interior staircase. "I would say that my home is to some extent mental in nature, because it is really a patchwork of homes that I have had and spaces where I have lived. My way of living—not just my home—is astonishingly simple. I stay home nearly all the time, and certainly I work a great deal, because I like to work. The studio is also a place with positive energy." Mendini works with his brother Francesco, an architect, with whom he founded the Atelier Mendini in 1989. "In any case, the separation of home and studio is fundamental because I change rhythms: my home is a space that allows me to think. There are times when I go downstairs to the studio, when it's empty, and work even on Sundays." When he is in Milan, he feels the need to find the right rhythms, to decontaminate himself from stress, from travel, from meals eaten on the run. And so he allows himself a small luxury: three times a week, a chef prepares macrobiotic meals for him, food designed to rebalance his organism, and delivers it to his

home. Home and studio are in a working-class neighborhood, on the outskirts of Milan, in a building that used to house the workers from a former factory: "Nowadays, there is an unusual blend of people, ethnicities, and cultures; it feels like living in the Bronx, in New York."

Mendini has Venetian origins, but he feels Milanese. What is his relationship with Milan like? "I think that the city has a great many faults, but I don't think that I could live anywhere else. The soil I sink my roots into is this smog, the grayness, the melancholy. It is also the center of gravity of my profession and so, since I am an Italian designer, I stay here, on the scene of the crime—even though I never go to exhibitions, I don't eat in restaurants, and I have no social life."

The apartment is very luminous, and the light is modulated by the colors of the walls: "I left the spaces broken up the way they were when I got here. I only painted the walls different colors because I like for every room to have a color of its own." An intense pink for his studio, light blue for the bedroom, yellow for the hallway; the living room is beige, and he is planning to repaint the kitchen in yellow, because it has a northern exposure and requires a warmer light.

In the apartment, there are prototypes that come and go, a sort of temporary warehouse. "When all is said and done, there's nothing special here," he says. "My ideal is that there should be very few things in my home. I would describe myself as an orderly person, with a tendency toward the *casa povera* (a reference to *art povera*). These little floor tiles, with tiny dots, seem as if they were predestined; they resemble my panel in the entrance hall, and so I would never remove them. I like a slightly monastic situation. It has to do with Zen, with meditation. Because of my profession, I am overwhelmed by too many images. I am introverted by nature, reluctant to engage in social interactions, but certain objects of mine are powerful and speak for me."

Mendini is a world-renowned architect. He was worked on urban design and furniture, interior decoration, objects, graphics, and interior decoration. And yet he says: "I don't know if I am an architect. I have always had a parallel interest in writing and criticism. For fifteen years, I devoted 80 percent of my time to journalism, so I might say that my overarching interest has always been literary to some extent." He talks about the time that Gio Ponti hired him as the editor-in-

chief of *Domus* as they shared a bottle of champagne. When asked if it is true that Alberto Alessi said to him: "I am hiring you to design my house because you are not an architect." He answers with some amusement: "It's true that I am considered to be someone who knows how to create houses where people are comfortable and contented, but I wouldn't know how to make a house for myself. Alessi used me as an anthropologist, as a psychologist. In those years, there was a sort of eclecticism in design, and that is a distinctive trait of my work as a designer."

How important is the component of playfulness and irony in Mendini's design? "Nowadays, especially in objects, there is a vulgar tendency to superluxury, an exaggerated ostentation of expense and consumption. I work for luxury brands as well, but I believe my saving grace is my irony, with the contradictions that I introduce and with the fact that I render my work problematic. This is not rhetoric, but I believe that there should be a more poetic relationship with objects, including functional objects. There is a sort of exaggeration of the functionality of objects. In some cases it is better when things function less well but are nicer-looking. An office chair should

Preceding pages, left: Alessandro Mendini in his bedroom. An untitled painting by Alessandro Mendini from 1966 hangs above a painting by Maria Morganti, 1990. Next to the bed is a chair from the Museo Bagatti Valsecchi, Mastrangelo, 1966. The metal wire chair is the *Pylon Chair* by Tom Dixon, Cappellini, 1994. The *Ecomimetico* (Ecomimetic) lamp is by Alessandro Mendini, 1998.
Preceding pages, right: The studio reflected in the *Diamante* (Diamond) mirror by Mendini for Glas, 1999.

Above: Details of three untitled paintings on wooden panels by Alessandro Mendini.
Opposite: To the left of the window stands a ceramic piece by Maria Christina Hamel, *Una zebra a pois* (A Polka Dot Zebra), Deruta, 1995. The lamp hanging from the ceiling is in Murano glass, designed by Mendini for Vnason, 2002. To the right of the window is the *Scimmia* (Monkey) table lamp by Anna Gili, 2001. On the far wall is a mirror, *Glas*, by Mendini for the Vitra Design Museum, 1999.

Preceding pages, left: In the living room, the lamp by Philippe Starck, *Cicatrices de Luxe 5* (Scars of Luxury 5), Flos, 2000; above the sofa, a painting on canvas by Mendini, Proust, 1990. In the corner, the *Lampada di Milo* (Milo Lamp) by Alessandro Mendini for Segno, 1988. Note the *San Leonardo* armchair, also by Mendini for Matteo Grassi, 1983. Over the door, an oil painting, *Albero* (Tree), by Mendini, 1999. The round *Nao* (Naos) table is also by Mendini for Lapis, 1992.

Preceding pages, right: an entire wall of the kitchen has been equipped with long shelves to display the entire series of the *100% Make Up* collection: one hundred vases decorated by one hundred artists and designers—including Mendini—who also designed the shape of the vase, Alessi Tendentze, 1992.

Left: The *Achernar* lamp, by Alessandro Mendini, in Murano glass, from the *Galassia* collection, Venini.
Opposite: A painting by Alex Mocika, *Lex Latex*, 1998. The *Poltrona Proust*, a piece of cult industrial design, by Alessandro Mendini. Notice the odd standing lamp, *Scolapasta* (Colander), designed by Philippe Starck for Alessi, 1966. The table was designed by Mendini and the aluminum chairs, American from the forties, are by Emeco.

Opposite: The residence is connected to the studio by a metal staircase painted yellow. In the foreground, note the chair created by YA/YA (Young Aspirations/Young Artists), 1990.
Above: On the walls of the studio, paintings by Alessandro Mendini, from 1996 to 1998. In the work space, as in the home, color predominates.

> " I like a slightly monastic situation. It has to do with Zen, with meditation. Because of my profession, I am overwhelmed by too many images. "

be functional, but a chair that you use to hang your clothes on can be a different matter."

Moving from one room to another, one sees a succession of surprising things: *oggetti poveri*, curious objects, objects of pure fantasy, furniture that serves a purpose, furniture that is sculpture, the writing desk of Gio Ponti, and a wire chair by Tom Dixon. "I always say that the object need not express its function and that imprecision is a quality." If there are any wardrobes, they aren't noticeable. In the bathroom, lined up in an orderly manner on a rack are a series of shoes, all of them black, all of them polished to a bright shine. Where does he keep his clothing? The answer is surprising. "I have never been capable of dressing myself properly. I didn't plan it out. I have the clothing that I need for the various circumstances of life, but I dress like a Milanese *borghese*, a member of the middle class."

Any personal memories of houses where you used to live? "The family home, where I was born. It was a beautiful house, built by the architect Portaluppi. My father had a collection of antique furniture from the eighteenth century, while my uncle who lived upstairs from us had a big collection of modern art, about two thousand paint-

ings: Severini, Balla, Depero, De Chrico, Morandi, and Sironi, which he later donated to the city of Milan. This had a considerable influence on me when I was a child: I lived between these two extremes, and I absorbed them both. In fact, I like tradition, too." In the Atelier Mendini there is the methodological tradition of the Renaissance. "Our mind-set is that of the Renaissance *bottega*, or workshop," says Mendini. He has just designed Alessi's new kitchen collection, consisting of four lines with variations in terms of materials and sizes. The lines are called *Geometrica* (Geometric), *Sinuosa* (Sinuous), *Agreste* (Rural), and *Trasparente* (Transparent). Very different from the simple cucina povera of Mendini's home. "I designed this kitchen myself, along with my carpenter, and I have used the table lots and lots of times, in my studio as well."

In the end, Mendini's real love is work: "I have no hobbies. I don't listen to music much, because I am a visual person more than an audio-visual person. I prefer silence. But now I'm interested in learning to navigate the Internet. No, not to design, to do research. I'm going to buy myself a computer."

> **"** *My bedroom is inside a cube in the center of a large, sixteenth-century room. I liked the idea of sleeping as if I were in a sleeping compartment on a passenger train, in a small and cozy space.* **"**

DINO GAVINA

Dino Gavina was born in Bologna in 1922. His first love was the visual arts, and from there he undertook his adventure in design, thanks to a meeting with Lucio Fontana in 1953. He is a manufacturer, an industrial designer, and the founder of the Gavina company, as well as a talent scout in the field of design. In 1960 he transformed his company, creating reproductions and collectors' items, producing pieces by Marcel Breuer, Man Ray, and Marcel Duchamp. He began to work with lamps for Flos, thanks to his remarkable partnership with Piergiacomo Castiglioni, the wizard of light. He produced lamps that have become icons of design, such as the Arco *lamp by Achille and Piergiacomo Castiglioni. He devoted himself to the production of multiple-production and modular furniture with Flos, Gavina, Simongavina, and Sirrah, the companies that he founded. He has created memorable collections:* Ultrarazionale, Ultramobile, *and* Metamobile. *World-renowned architects and artists have worked with Gavina: from Carlo Scarpa, Marcel Breuer, and Marcel Duchamp to Man Ray, the Castiglioni brothers, and Kazuhide Takahama. In 1969 he founded, with Carlo Scarpa and Cesare Cassina, the Centro Duchamp cultural association.*

Dino Gavina lives in Bologna, in an apartment in a sixteenth-century *palazzo*. The apartment was originally split up into many rooms, but Gavina eliminated all the walls and made it into an open space. It has high ceilings, imposing doors of sixteenth-century proportions, and windows that allow light to flood in. His home is filled with objects that are connected to his memories of friendships, emotions, and important encounters. They reflect his great love of art and of books, which fill every corner. Every object, every piece of furniture tells of his tireless passion for design.

His adventure in design began with his great love of art and, in particular, with a meeting with Lucio Fontana in 1953. Fontana became one of Dino Gavina's close friends because Gavina loved art, and he would go to Milan frequently to see exhibitions and in time he became acquainted with many contemporary artists. "I had built a small writing desk for Fontana, to use in his studio in Corso Monforte. He really liked it, and he asked me: "Why don't you come live in Milan? You could work with the architects here. They're all nice guys." He took me with him to the Triennale, and there I made the acquaintance of Piergiacomo Castiglioni, whom I still consider the greatest

Italian designer; I also met Carlo De Carli, Carlo Mollino, Marco Zanuso, and Ignazio Gardella." These were memorable meetings for Dino Gavina, an "enlightened" entrepreneur, a designer, and a full-fledged talent scout who intuited at a glance the potential of individuals and situations; he created a unique, never-to-be-repeated phenomenon in the history of Italian design.

In the fifties, Gavina had an upholstery store and workshop in Bologna and he had already produced the *Tripolina* chair, his first product conceived for mass production and an homage to the Maestri Anonimi: "If I think back on it, this chair is the most beautiful thing I have ever made. It is simple, it's made of nothing, really. It's just an animal hide draped over four sticks, but it is comfortable and convenient, and it fits in all kinds of spaces." The young Milanese architects of the postwar years were attempting to establish a dialogue with the Italian manufacturers of the period, and they leapt at the opportunity to design objects for him. "The word *design* had not yet come into circulation, but there was lots of enthusiasm, it all remained to be invented, it all remained to be discovered. That truly was design. The design that you see nowadays is all just a bluff."

" I made furniture that
was neither furniture
nor painting nor
sculpture, but which
had a strong
personality: it was
a specific sign, a
particular presence
in the context
of furnishing or
interior decoration. "

Gavina threw himself headlong into the undertakings that he believed in. His career path, which was uphill every step of the way, certainly left a mark in the sector of furnishings: with such memorable initiatives as, in 1968, *Ultrarazionale* (literally, "ultra-rational," rational furniture that went well beyond Rationalism and took into account elements that are not part of Rationalism, such as the type of material and its thickness); in 1971, *Ultramobile* (in Italian, a play on words involving the term "*mobile,*" which means both movable and furniture: this was mass-produced furniture that referenced art, as if the pieces were multiples by famous artists); in 1974, *Metamobile* (a genuine revolution against expensive designer furniture, with a proposal of simple and very affordable furniture). In addition to creating these objects, he founded companies that would become important names in the history of design: Gavina, in 1960; Flos, in 1961; and Simongavina and Sirrah, in 1974.

At the beginning of the sixties, Gavina left for New York, where he presented himself at the studio of Marcel Breuer. He did not know a word of English or German. But he knew Breuer's tubular furniture from the twenties, and he wanted to manufacture furniture designed by the Bauhaus maestro. "I went back to Bologna with a number of his designs, including the *Wassily* chair, from 1925, which I named after Wassily Kandinsky, who was the first to buy the prototype. I saw this chair in Kandinsky's house when I went to have tea with his wife, Nina." Gavina put it back into production, in 1960.

In Gavina's home, there are many lamps that he produced for Flos; he had an extraordinary partnership and friendship with Piergiacomo Castiglioni, who—along with his brother Achille—designed a number of memorable lamps that have become icons of Italian design, such as the *Toio*, the *Taccia*, and the *Arco*, in 1962, the last being one of the most extensively copied pieces of design on earth. At the request of Dino Gavina, the Castiglioni brothers also designed an armchair, the *Sanluca*, reminiscent of the Futurist sculptures of Boccioni. Memories emerge in Dino Gavina's impassioned and detailed accounts and he is a generous fount of anecdotes. As one wanders through his home, one becomes curious about the numerous objects that populate and enliven the apartment and bridge the area between art and design. Gavina says that there isn't that much in his house,

Preceding pages, left: Dino Gavina on the *Mantilla* sofa, designed by Kazuhide Takahama for Simongavina, 1974. On the *Dijuna* café table by Takahama is a creation by Giacomo Balla, a chrome-plated metal flower, produced by the Centro Duchamp. On top of the bookcase is a painting by Guido Cagnacci.
Preceding pages, right: On top of the cube that contains his sleeping area is a giant word, "Naviga" (Navigate), an anagram of his surname, Gavina, by the artist Sabato Angero.

Above: The corridor with bookcases designed by Carlo Scarpa, the *Sanluca* armchair by the Castiglioni brothers, and a café table by Meret Oppenheim, all produced by Gavina. In front of the armchair sits a large terra-cotta bowl by Lucio Fontana, and near the window is a sculpture by Carlo Scarpa made of steel with a golden luminescence. On the far wall is a painting of a woman with a dove, by Antiveduto Grammatica, 1610.
Opposite: In the study is a piece from the *Ultramobile* collection, *Margareta*, by Gavina. Formerly a bin for holding grain, it was cut open and cast in bronze to form a throne/chair. Atop the bookcase is a portrait of Gavina by the Neapolitan artist Sabato Angero, who creates his works by burning paper.

but what's there fits well. All the things that surround him are linked to the emotions surrounding a meeting or a discovery. His home is one long story. The bedroom is set within a cube, at the center of a grand hall with the proportions of the sixteenth century. It is like a room set within another room: "I liked the idea of sleeping as if I were in a sleeping compartment on a passenger train, in a small and cozy space." The bathroom is upstairs and it is reached by climbing up a steep staircase of staggered steps that Gavina, at the age of eighty-three, climbs with surprising agility. "At night, I don't even need to turn on the light." Hanging on the walls are paintings, drawings, sketches, both new artworks and antiques because, as he says, "artworks never age." The secret of all this sprightly agility is also the bicycle that he keeps in his house, next to the sofa. He bikes every day and even takes part in races: he recently participated in the one-hundred-kilometer (sixty-mile) "Bologna-Comacchio" race, joining the other racers to cover just the last thirty kilometers (twenty miles).

Also quite memorable was his meeting with Carlo Scarpa, who designed a table in glossy lacquer for him. "I had guessed that Scarpa would be fascinated by this material, lacquer, which comes

from China. I had found a way to make it on an industrial basis. But I knew that Scarpa was not interested in design, so I provoked him. I made a table and showed it to him. He immediately changed the design." This led to the creation of the *Orseolo* table.

But his most original operation was the production of the extraordinary pieces of furniture objects that lay midway between art and mass production, which Gavina was able to produce thanks to his friendships in the field of art. One example was Man Ray's creation *Les grands trans-Parents*, an artistic mirror that Gavina mass-produced at a truly affordable price; another was an object inspired by the work of Brancusi. "I made furniture that was neither furniture nor painting nor sculpture, but which had a strong personality: it was a specific sign, a particular presence in the context of furnishing or interior decoration. Those who bought them, without even realizing it, wound up with an artwork in their home," says Gavina.

Many of Dino Gavina's friends are no longer alive. The *ragazzi milanesi*—the young Milanese architects who were pioneers of Italian design—are now world famous, and much of the credit for that goes to him.

Preceding pages: The study, spacious and luminous, with the *Orseolo* table designed for Gavina by Carlo Scarpa, in 1972. In the foreground, the *Toio* floor lamp, and on the table, the *Taccia* lamp, both designed by Achille and Piergiacomo Castiglioni for Flos, 1962. At the far end of the room, on top of the *Kaidan* dresser, designed by Takahama in 1962, is the *Saori* lamp, an homage by the Japanese designer to Lucio Fontana. On the right is the work of a great artist, Domenico Rambelli.

Above, left: Designed by Carlo Scarpa, a bizarre staircase made up of high, offset, staggered steps leads to the bathroom. On the wall, the *Light Ball* appliqué, designed by Achille and Piergiacomo Castiglioni for Flos, and next to it, a "rayograph" by Man Ray and a painting by the artist Andrea Boyer.
Above, right: A room inside another room, the cube contains a small bedroom and a wardrobe. On the wall of the cube is a Sienese painting of an angel from the sixteenth century.
Opposite: The interior of the cube is furnished sparely, a sliding door/wall made of glass isolates its occupant from the rest of the room.

" Memories? The memories of a lifetime, like a city, which is the stratification of the memory of a people; likewise a house is the stratification of personal memories, memories of family and people. "

MARIO
BELLINI

The Milanese architect Mario Bellini's international fame is linked both to his vast body of work as an industrial designer (in 1987 the Museum of Modern Art in New York devoted a major exhibition to his work), and to his numerous architectural projects. Among his most important projects, aside from the office machinery, chairs, and the objects (designed for Olivetti, Cassina, B & B, Vitra, Rosenthal, Yamaha, and others), are the Portello sector of the Milan Fair, the Centro esposizioni e congressi (conference and exhibition center) of Villa Erba on Lake Como, the Tokyo Design Center, the headquarters of Natuzzi America, and the new fair district in Essen, Germany. Among his most recent successes are three prestigious commissions: the National Gallery of Victoria, in Melbourne, Australia, the new Central Library and Theater in Turin, and the Department of Islamic Arts at the Louvre in Paris. Mario Bellini was the editor-in-chief of the magazine Domus from 1986 to 1991. He has delivered lectures and taught courses around the world and has won many prizes and awards for his work as an industrial designer and architect. In 2005, the President of the Republic of Italy conferred upon him the national Medal of Honor for his work. In 2007 the Milan Triennale will devote a major retrospective show to his work.

It might seem odd, but Mario Bellini explains that one of the reasons he chose his current home is the marvelous garden it overlooks. The element of greenery is very important to him. Greenery and silence: a true privilege in the heart of Milan, in the historic center where the palazzi conceal astonishing courtyards and gardens of rare beauty. The garden of his residence in the Via Borgonuovo is set between the general headquarters of Giorgio Armani and the Brera Orto Botanico, or Botanical Gardens, a tiny corner filled with rare plants.

The palazzo, originally Neoclassical in style, in which the architect Bellini lives, has vaulted ceilings, which were frescoed in the thirties at the behest of the Milanese architect Piero Portaluppi. "Let's say that a home should not be banal and that it should have a great quality of density and a certain capacity for expression. This house is a space of great quality: it has a structure that Portaluppi created by stitching together two nineteenth-century buildings, and so it has vaults and pseudo-classical decorative motifs, but they are from the thirties. It has thick walls and large arched windows that overlook a historic garden which adjoins the Botanical Gardens; there is a

view of the Torre dell'Astronomo, or astronomical observatory, of Brera." A special place therefore. Milanese by birth, Mario Bellini says that he is very fond of the center of his city. "I like living in the historic center because it is dense with memory and significance: theaters, stores, restaurants, cafés, bookshops, it's all concentrated here in the center: there always seems to be something in the process of being transformed, something changing, and you can feel the pulse of the evolution of fashions and times over the years."

While the original architectural structure is important, equally important are the modifications that Mario Bellini has carried out over the years. Bellini has lived in this house for twenty-five years, and he has renovated it three times. In the eighties, the first renovation was done with his friend the architect Gae Aulenti, creating a wall-sized bookshelf that stretches up two stories holding thousands of volumes. "If I had not been an architect and an industrial designer, I would probably have been a poet and a writer," says Mario Bellini who—when he was the editor-in-chief of the visionary architecture magazine Domus—wrote no fewer than sixty-five publisher's letters, all genuine short essays, written at

night, because during the day he needed to tend to his work as an architect. Now he is preparing a book that will contain all his writings and reflections on architecture and the city. He has some surprising theories about design: "'Design' is a term of jargon that has given rise to more than a few historic and cultural misunderstandings; humanity has always designed objects of everyday use, machinery, tools, chairs, and furnishings, and I am not particularly impressed by the fact that nowadays we have decided to refer to all that as 'design.'"

The steps that run around the library are protected by a structure of high-tech turquoise-colored tubing. But this aspect of the renovation falls into the background as soon as one climbs to the second floor, the more private section of the house, and enters a surprising space. The latest renovation, dating back two or three years, was the work of David Tremlett, an English artist hired by Bellini to do frescoes on the upper story, where the dining room, kitchen, and bedrooms are located. The result is an intense chromatic effect with Mediterranean colors, very different form the muted hues of Portaluppi's frescoes. A whiplash of pure energy. "Tremlett's frescoes fit

perfectly in this space. They have a remarkable evocative capacity. Nothing has been the same since Tremlett did this series of paintings; the work he did had a decisive and surprising effect," says Bellini. "The house has a historic character, of great communicative efficacy, which subsequent interventions have preserved and made more powerful while emphasizing its figurative, emotional, and spatial effects."

Climbing to the second floor is a moving experience, like entering a canvas of contemporary abstract art. The entire space has become a work of art. One is enveloped by the powerful strokes of Tremlett's painting and drawn into a kaleidoscopic fresco of colored geometries. One moves in an unusual dimension, because the fresco-graffiti extends from the ceiling to the pillars and the walls. Even if Tremlett's pictorial narrative overwhelms everything else, there are pieces of design that stand out for their personality—a café table by Ron Arad and a large marble table that Bellini created for Cassina, rightly called *Colonnato* (Colonnade), surrounded by the *Vol-au-Vent* chairs designed by Bellini for B & B— and find an appropriate setting in this space. Also on the upper floor is a large sixteenth-century

Preceding pages, left: Mario Bellini standing in front of a silver-colored panel at the entrance of his Milanese home. To his right is the *Teatrino scientifico* (Little Scientific Theater) by Aldo Rossi, 1978. *Le strutture tremano* (The Structures Tremble), designed by Ettore Sottsass for Alchimia, 1979, stands on the other side of the entrance. In the adjoining room are the *Spartana* (Spartan Woman) chairs by Hans Coray, produced by Zanotta.

Preceding pages, right: The staircase that leads to the upper story, with an unusual table by Carlo Mollino and the canvas *Reclining Nude* by Ubaldo Oppi, 1930.

Above, left: A mirrored dressing table attributed to Gio Ponti from the forties. Above it is a painting from the thirties, *L'operaia* (Female Laborer) by Cagnaccio di San Pietro.

Above, right: A table covered with parchment, from the forties, with a collection of Murano glass and ceramics. The painting *Bambini che giocano* (Children at Play) is by Cagnaccio di San Pietro, 1925. Next to the table stands a floor lamp from the fifties by Angelo Lelii for Arredoluce.

Opposite: On the dressing table, a sequence of glass items, *Colpi di vento* (Gusts of Wind), by Fulvio Bianconi for Venini.

Opposite: The living room with a frescoed vaulted ceiling and a large sixteenth-century Roman fireplace. On the far wall, on the left, the painting *Double Portrait* by Felice Casorati, 1921, and on the right, the painting *The Architect* by Mario Sironi, 1922. Next to the sofa that faces the fireplace, an original round coffee table by Alvar Aalto for Artek. In the foreground, the *La Basilica* table by Mario Bellini for Cassina, 1976, with *Cherner Chair* seats by Norman Cherner, 1958. The living room faces a beautiful garden.

Above: The white *George* sofas are by Antonio Citterio for B & B Italia. The sculptural stereo speakers are by Avant-Garde Acoustics. The standing lamps are from the thirties and forties. On the balustrade are the sketches for the painted narrative of frescoes on the upper story, created by David Tremlett.

fireplace, and another fireplace with a plaster graffito, set in a frame of Art Deco marble, in the bedroom. Sixteenth-century fireplaces and Aubusson tapestries confer upon the rooms a note of refinement that is reminiscent of certain details of a castle. It is a theatrical house, one might even say "an official reception setting," but Bellini responds that it is a highly functional and comfortable house "where children grew up, my four children."

An extraordinary mix of pieces—rare, exquisite, dating from diverse eras and boasting various styles—can be found throughout the house. The entrance is only a passageway, but it has a remarkable story to tell with artworks by Aldo Rossi, Ettore Sottsass, a mirrored console by Gio Ponti from the forties, and *After the Orgy*, a painting by Cagnaccio di San Pietro from 1920. Collections of Venini glass and a gallery of artwork line the walls, including canvases from the thirties by Mario Sironi, Mario Broglio, Ubaldo Oppi, and Felice Casorati. In order to reach the living room, one must go through a portal with steps and a sculpture by Arturo Martini, *La pisana*, then pass under a monumental archway to enter a large room filled with light.

The room that looks out over the garden has large white sofas gathered around a sixteenth-century fireplace. Bellini's passion for music is documented by a *Bolidist* (neo-Futuristic) stereo system and a grand piano. Everywhere are Indian carpets, dhurries, with geometric patterns and dusty colors—pink, pastel green, ivory—that harmonize with the old frescoes. "Here, there are objects, furniture, paintings, signs that reflect my tastes and my curiosities. Memories? The memories of a lifetime, like a city, which is the stratification of the memory of a people; likewise a house is the stratification of personal memories, memories of family and people. My children no longer live at home, my wife is no longer with us, but the echo of their presence remains."

Mario Bellini, after a fortunate and dizzyingly rapid debut as an industrial designer, winning eight Golden Compass awards for his popular items for Cassina, B & B, and Olivetti, has been working for the past twenty-five years primarily on architectural projects around the world. "In my entire professional life, I believe that I never did anything just for the work, but only for the satisfaction and for creative happiness. Each project is a challenge and a new adventure."

Opposite: The library, with a pear-wood staircase and turquoise-blue painted railing structure, built in 1984 to plans by Mario Bellini and Gae Aulenti. On the wall above the first-level bookcase is *Raccolta del legno* (Gathering Wood), a painting by Gorni.
Right: In the foreground, the *CAB* armchairs by Mario Bellini for Cassina, 1977. *Colonnato* (Colonnade) marble table, by Bellini for Cassina, 1977, with the *Vol-au-Vent* chairs also by Bellini but for B & B Italia, 2001. On the walls and on the ceilings, frescoes by David Tremlett.

Overleaf, left: On the marble table, a collection of vases, *Sogni Infranti* (Shattered Dreams), by Mario Bellini for Venini, 1992.
Overleaf, right: The fresco on the ceiling is reflected in a silver bowl from the forties.

Above, left: Next to a fireplace in the bedroom, the *La chaise*, 1948, a chair by Charles and Ray Eames.
Above, right: Above the bed, a sixteenth-century Aubusson tapestry depicting King David and Bathsheba conceals the door leading to the hallway and bathroom. The chairs are by Norman Cherner for Plycraft, 1948.
Opposite: This exceedingly refined bathroom features exquisite materials, such as the marble sink, designed by Bellini for UPGroup. The *S-Chair* is by Tom Dixon for Cappellini.

" I am convinced that furnishing should not invade one's life or complicate it.
I am only interested in the quality of the space where I live, where I move. "

ETTORE
SOTTSASS

Ettore Sottsass was born in Innsbruck, Austria, in 1917. He took his degree in architecture at the Politecnico, or Polytechnic University, of Turin in 1939, and he began his career in Milan, where he opened his own studio in 1947. In the fifties he began working with Olivetti and designed typewriters, electronic calculators (Golden Compass award in 1970), and a system of office furniture. This collaboration was to last for over thirty years. One of his typewriters, the Valentine, made of red plastic, from 1969, is a cult design object. From 1966 to 1972 he was an active protagonist of Radical Design, which promoted industrial design as a tool of social criticism; in the sixties, he designed furniture for Poltronova and was a member of the Alchimia group. In 1981 he founded, with other world-renowned architects, the Memphis group, whose furniture became design icons. Later, Sottsass worked with such art galleries as the Blum Helman Gallery in New York and the Mourmans Gallery. Sottsass Associati, founded in 1980, is still active in Milan. His design projects are featured in the permanent collections of the most important museums in the world—the Museum of Modern Art in New York, the Centre Pompidou in Paris, and the Victoria & Albert Museum in London, among others.

The Milanese apartment of Ettore Sottsass, the guru of international design and the founder of the Memphis group, the movement that revolutionized contemporary industrial design by placing feelings and emotions ahead of the function of objects, is a simple and very luminous space. There is not much furniture, and the pieces that are there are essential, designed by Sottsass himself, who lives here with his companion, Barbara Radice. "We have more objects than we do furniture," he says. "Our lives are described by the little things. It is the sensory aspects that count: the colors, the sounds, the weights, the distances, the space, and the light—all things that we perceive with our senses. In our homes, there are memories that travel continuously through the environments. There are special smells: certain houses are scented. Certain houses smell of broth or apples, like the house where I was a child in Trentino."

Sottsass claims that this is true for design as well: sensory design has a certain color, a certain weight, a certain depth… He describes developing this idea of sensory design in the mountains, in Innsbruck, where he was born to a father from Trent: "As a child I was very lucky because I grew up in the forests, in the meadows: I didn't think I

existed, I could 'feel' that I existed. I could sense odors, flavors, heat, cold, the seasons." And now Sottsass continues to believe that living in a house means perceiving space with your senses.

This apartment is made up of memories more than of objects. Memories of friends, memories of trips, small objects picked up here and there—not out of a mania for owning things but for the pleasure of reliving certain emotions. Ettore and Barbara have similar tastes: they love certain forms of simple folk art, small and inexpensive objects. They love art, and on the wall are drawings by Peter Halley, Mimmo Paladino, old drawings by Sottsass, and paintings by the artist Mario Radice, Barbara's father. The large painting on paper is a gift from their friend Francesco Clemente: even though it has been well smoothed out and framed, you can still see where it was folded. Sottsass folded it to bring it back from the United States, where he had gone to pay a call on the artist.

Sottsass would fill the apartment up with books: his books are neatly lined up on the shelves of a bookcase made out of pearwood, which he designed himself; it is very light because the shelves are only half an inch thick. "Endless

books—we just keep buying them. Then there is the problem of CDs, which we didn't use to have to deal with, and then of course records, which are one of Barbara's memories because I never owned any."

The important thing about this apartment is the sense of space and scale, even though the apartment is not really that big. Ettore says that he is comfortable in this space, and that emptiness is important: "Here, for instance, we are obsessed with fullness. There is an archive that we have been working on: over the years I have collected articles, calendars, projects, just lots and lots of stuff... I tend to hold on to things while Barbara, fortunately, tends to select. I would like to keep everything because I am afraid of the passage of time, and in reality of course I am afraid of death, like everybody. Something that disappears is gone forever. I am frightened by things that are definitive."

Sottsass shows me a little statuette that a Chinese friend gave him: "It depicts a high court official who resembles me; lots of people ask me if it's a portrait of me!" Then, a café table designed in 1948: "I went to a lacquerer, who would always make fake eighteenth-century

armoires, and gilt picture frames, and all that sort of stuff. It was very odd for Turin, which is a very conservative city. We always remember his famous phrase: 'Architect Sottsass, when you don't know what to do, just put in a mirror, and that always works!'"

The space is emphasized by the color, which has a certain importance. The living room is a squarish room, larger than a room in a normal apartment: "I immediately liked this very much. In the middle of the day there is a beautiful light. There is a hallway but it is very short and it leads straight here. There are no rooms on either side of it. All we needed to do was break up the corridor with a piece of furniture: over there, where you pass through, I used a slightly daring green. Over here where we live, I used this hazelnut color, a little bit warmer." Sottsass is convinced that furnishing should not invade a life or complicate it; he says that he is especially interested in the quality of the space where he lives, where he moves. Furniture should be simple and functional: large tables, comfortable chairs. And then there are objects that are not functional, and it seems that they are there only to decorate. Instead, they are there to keep us company, too,

Preceding pages, left: A portrait of Ettore Sottsass.
Preceding pages, right: A view of the living room with its hazelnut-colored walls. In the living room the protagonist is the large canvas, *The Four Corners*, by Francesco Clemente, a tempera on paper that was a gift from the artist to the owners of the apartment.

Above, left: A niche in the wall houses a Buddha, who protects the apartment.
Above, right: In the entrance corridor, the walls are painted in various shades of green.
Opposite: In front of the canvas by Francesco Clemente is a dark blue table by Ettore Sottsass and an aluminum Navy Chair from the forties, produced by the American company Emeco.

to make us feel okay. A red plaster horn, a stat-uette of Buddha that protects the home, a painted basket full of pomegranates, a protective Japanese tiger, two small Iranian vases, a little Chinese cage with singing birds. "We are inter-ested in Asian cultures, and we are attracted by different ways of perceiving space, color, and silence."

For someone like him, who has traveled so much, has his home been a point of reference? "A home is a point of reference because what is in your home is your own history. It reflects the way you live. I don't know why, but I have always been curious to see what there is outside of my home, on the other side of my garden wall, and so I have traveled a great deal. But I never felt that I was a nomad. I was going in search of some-thing: travel was a job, a quest, an experiment. I never looked on it as a means of escape or a change in my situation."

He called himself Sottsass Junior to differen-tiate himself from his father, the architect Ettore Sottsass. "My father, an architect, wanted me to be an architect: he was a noble man, not by descent or official status, but in the way he lived. I became an architect and I did lots of design. I

designed architecture for private homes. Clearly I wasn't very good at negotiating with banks and other institutions. So I could say that I am a theo-retical architect. I have designed some interesting houses, but I've never designed a skyscraper or a museum. But I have thought about architecture quite a bit, what it is and what it means. In the meanwhile, people live in architecture, unlike any other form of art. It is the design of a setting in which we live. It is not the façade or the elevation that counts: that's construction. Out of a thou-sand buildings in a city, if you're lucky, ten of them might also be pieces of architecture. As an architect I took care to design a comfortable, flex-ible place where it is possible to keep in mind the orientation, the landscape, the winds, the rains, and—on the interior—the passageways, the win-dows and the walls, and then place life inside it. I wound up describing myself as a theoretical designer, too, because I think about design a lot. At first, Memphis was fun. We were trying to understand what was happening and no one knew what to do. But there was lots of curiosity, enthusiasm, and talent among the young people who were following me, as well. And a funda-mental thing kept us going: our dreams."

Preceding pages, left: A bookcase over the sofa con-tains souvenirs from various trips and a scale model of the *Carlton* bookcase designed by Sottsass, from the Memphis collection. The photograph of Ettore and Barbara is by David Hamilton. Books are every-where in the home of Ettore Sottsass, along with items that are linked to friends or trips, and small oriental objects to protect the home.
Preceding pages, right: On the white table in Corian in the living room, designed by Sottsass, stand vases full of fresh flowers, a natural element that softens the rigor of the setting.

Above: In the bedroom, the *Asteroide* (Asteroid) lamp, designed by Sottsass for Poltronova, 1968; the table is a one-off designed by Sottsass for Zanotta; the dresser is a prototype.
Opposite: Behind the bed, a long shelf runs along the wall, featuring books and objects. The head-board of the bed fits under the shelf and also serves as a cabinet; it was designed by Sottsass, made of white laminate with forms in pearwood. Atop the green-lacquered wooden sculpture stand a number of glass items from the Memphis collection, all by Ettore Sottsass.

" *This house has a certain quality of self-sufficiency, and the alternative ideas of a house as a small city and the city as a large house. This large house is like a small city, the large living room or great hall is the exterior, the 'field' where I work is also the coldest place. Often I stay at home for days at a time, simply walking through my house, playing my piano, reading, or drawing.* "

MASSIMO
SCOLARI

Massimo Scolari lives and works in Venice. He took his degree in architecture at the Politecnico, or Polytechnic University of Milan in 1969 and was immediately hired as a member of the editorial staff of Controspazio *and as the appointed assistant lecturer for Aldo Rossi's university course. In 1973 he became an adjunct professor, teaching the history of architecture in the department of architecture at the University of Palermo and a professor of industrial design at the Istituto Universitario in Venice. He resigned from the university in 2000. He was the Arthur Rotch Visiting Professor at Harvard University from 1986 to 1988; a visiting professor at the Royal College of Art in London in 1983 and at the Royal Danish Academy in Copenhagen in 1993. He has been an editor for* Controspazio, Lotus, *and* Casabella, *and he supervised the architecture series for the publisher Franco Angeli Editore, from 1973 to 1988. He was the editor of arts, architecture, and music for* Eidos *from 1988 until 1995. In 2005 he published, for Marsilio,* Disegno obliquo, *a collection of his studies on representation. He created installations for the Milan Triennale, the Venice Biennale, and for the Museo Palladio in Vicenza. His works have been exhibited in the United States, Europe, and Japan and are in the permanent collections of*

The home of Massimo Scolari, in Venice, is near the Arsenal, in an area that Venetians consider out of the way, far from the crowds of tourists. It is a place that seems suspended in time, silent, almost motionless. This is an ideal location for an artist like Scolari, who paints fantastic cities, desert landscapes, and futuristic architecture. He is a painter, a sculptor, a writer, and a designer of pieces of furniture that are small architectural projects, but he considers himself an artist above all. "Architecture has been a theme in my painting, and it gave me a mental formation for the design that I do, including furniture design. But art and painting are central to my life." He has chosen to live far from the circuits of design in Milan, because, he says, he has never been fond of socializing.

The *palazzo* where Scolari lives was, in the seventeenth century, the residence of Giovanni Sagredo, a member of an aristocratic Venetian family that imported wood from the Cadore area, as documented by the beams the ceilings. Sagredo was the Venetian ambassador to Paris, London, and Vienna. "We know there was a portrait of the owner in the library, his coat of arms is in the entrance hall, with the three fleurs-de-lys of France, conceded to Giovanni Sagredo by Louis

XIV." When Scolari saw the building for the first time, it was in terrible shape, "a longtime home to hundreds of pigeons." He immediately intuited that this was the house of his life, and he committed to a lengthy and expensive renovation. All of the walls, which were made of *marmorino*, were restored to their age-old magnificence. Now the building is as it must have looked in the seventeenth century. The *stanzone*, or great room, overlooking the Campo della Celestia, boasts extraordinary cherrywood bookcases that Scolari had custom built. The large library is perhaps the room where Massimo Scolari spends most of his time. A special room with an evocative atmosphere and fascinating light. Along the entire upper part of the library, runs a decoration made of stucco in relief, an original frieze from the seventeenth century.

According to Scolari, the fundamental elements of a home are space, light, and a soul. "The spirit of a place counts a great deal: a house should have a history, a significance. I have always lived and worked in settings that were not much bigger than a hundred square meters (about a thousand square feet). My house in Asolo was literally covered with books, including in the bathroom. At a

the Museum of Modern Art in New York, the
Deutsches Architektur Museum in Frankfurt, and
the Teheran Museum of Modern Art. Since 1989
he has designed furniture for Giorgetti. In 2006
he was invited to Yale University as the Davenport
Visiting Professor.

Previous pages, left: Massimo Scolari at his worktable
in the library. Behind him is a replica of a Hellenistic
head, made by the British Museum.
Previous pages, right: The *palazzo* in which, on the
main floor, or *piano nobile*, Scolari lives.

Opposite: In a corner of the living room, an odd piece
of furniture, from a sacristy for sacred vestments,
with deep drawers where Scolari keeps his drawings,
watercolors, and sheets of paper. On the easel is an
unfinished oil painting by Massimo Scolari.
Above: On the walls of the living room are paintings
from the late nineteenth and early twentieth centuries, with landscapes in the Dolomites. The black
leather armchair is by Charles and Ray Eames. On the
right, the door that leads to the library: the statue is
a plaster cast of Venus from the nineteenth century.

certain point I felt that I needed to have space
around me, even if my 'abhorrence of a vacuum'
tends continuously to fill that space up."

In the various rooms, we can read the history
of Massimo Scolari the painter: actually, one does-
not see many of his paintings in the house. The
canvas *L'ultima città conosciuta* hangs in the living
room, and maybe a work in progress can be found
on an easel. In the house one can also follow his
career as an industrial designer. The pieces of
furniture he designed for Giorgetti are small mas-
terpieces of cabinetmaking, elegance and proportion. He claims that he would gladly give up all the
furniture that he has designed, but not his
antiques. "Design is there when a piece of furniture is useful and beautiful, and it's beautiful if it
corresponds to the appropriate level of utility."

The enormous hall—which stands before the
library—should be explored at leisure. Here one
discovers the secrets of the master of the house:
the presence of a Steinway grand piano reveals
that he is also a musician. Model airplanes tell us
about his love of flying. "Painting is my work and
flying is my passion. I imagine that in some way,
music, flying, and reading must all interact when
you produce something with any technique at all."

In the library, there is a small mummified peregrine falcon, documenting his love for Egypt,
where he has traveled repeatedly to study the
depiction in ancient Egypt, especially in Saqqara.
He also took part in the competition for the design
of the Grand Egyptian Museum in Cairo.

Scolari says he has no sentimental ties to
Venice. "I have always thought that what counts
in a city, more than the architecture, are the people. A person moves around, following his friendships and emotional ties, not seeking out certain
stones." He was born in Novi Ligure, where his
family had been evacuated during World War II,
and as a child he spent two years in Switzerland.
"In the land of chocolate, I began to feel a certain
sense of indifference to places. And so I felt no
regrets when, in order to flee the social life of
Milan in the eighties, I went to live in Asolo. I have
always traveled a great deal, so I don't particularly
feel Milanese or Venetian, much less Asolan."
What he loves about Venice is the light and the
silence. "This is a truly modern city: there are no
outskirts. It has two airports. There are no noisy
cars, and you can enjoy a comforting silence. The
large *palazzi* are scattered throughout the city and
mingle with ordinary houses."

When asked how important the spectacular, theatrical element is to him in a home, he replies: "Sometimes Venice is just too beautiful, and that can be difficult to accept. Even here in this house, there are conditions of light in the autumn that can cause a sense of torment at the overwhelming excess of beauty." The rooms are filled with memories, recollections that surround him and often take concrete form in objects. Some are beautiful, others are simple but intense. His favorite corner? "I have not yet found the place where creative energies are optimized. I suspect in the kitchen, but the library has its potential. This house has a certain quality of self-sufficiency, and the alternative ideas of a house as a small city and the city as a large house. This large house is like a small city, the large living room or great hall is the exterior, the 'field' where I work is also the coldest place. Often I stay at home for days at a time, simply walking through my house, playing my piano, reading, or drawing."

Is this his last and permanent home? "The voyage continues but I have the impression that this home really could be *L'ultima città conosciuta*."

❝ *Sometimes Venice is just too beautiful, and that can be difficult to accept. Even here in this house, there are conditions of light in the autumn that can cause a sense of torment at the overwhelming excess of beauty.* **❞**

Preceding pages: In the living room, a vitrine contains a collection of *objets trouvés* from the second half of the nineteenth century. The piece of furniture in the center is a British glass-front bookcase from the first half of the nineteenth century, and it contains pigments, little bottles of paint, and brushes. Between the two pieces of furniture, set on a leather armchair, is a veiled statue of a woman that was part of an installation, *Oltre il cielo* (Beyond the Sky) at the Venice Biennale of 1984.

Right: A view of the great hall-qua-atelier with drawing boards in every corner; the chair in the foreground is a Thonet. On the right, beneath the mirror, is a Biedermeier writing desk. In front of the window is the *Sagredo* table, designed by Massimo Scolari for Giorgetti. The hall has four doors with cornices made of Istrian stone, which lead to four different rooms. The wooden ceiling dates from the seventeenth century and the style of flooring is typical of Venice.

Opposite: The entrance to the library, with a large writing desk in the middle of the room, designed by Massimo Scolari. The chair is a walnut Biedermeier piece. Over the writing desk is the *Arco* (Arc) lamp by Achille Castiglioni for Flos. The sculpture of Venus in the foreground is a plaster cast from the nineteenth century.

Above: A corner of the living room. The *Sagredo* table, designed by Massimo Scolari for Giorgetti, has a sliding top that covers receptacles that can be used as drawers. The *Ubea* chair and the *Spring* armchair are by Massimo Scolari and are produced by Giorgetti. The lamp and the table to the left of the doorway, date from the thirties. On the round table is a model by Léon Krier; on the small bookcase is a scale model of Noah's Ark, part of *Il progetto domestico*, an exhibition at the Milan Triennale, in 1986. Through the doorway is the kitchen with furniture designed by Massimo Scolari. The hanging lamp is by Poul Henningsen for Poulsen, 1957.

Overleaf, left: On a walnut table from Venice, dating to the first half of the nineteenth century, are a series of Chinese vases and a terra-cotta scale model of a Chinese country house. On the wall are two round frames containing an agate and a green jasper; between them is a collection of swatches of watercolors by Windsor & Newton; to the right, a late-nineteenth-century French painting.

Overleaf, right: A piece of Venetian walnut furniture from the first half of the nineteenth century contains a collection of drawing tools and compasses from the period ranging from the seventeenth century to the nineteenth century.

Second overleaf, left: The library with four cherrywood bookcases designed by Scolari for this room, each four meters tall. The writing desk next to the bookcase is Danish, from the sixties. The writing desk in the middle of the room was designed by Massimo Scolari. Atop the table is the *Arco* (Arc) lamp by Achille Castiglioni for Flos. The little parlor near the windows has *Liba* armchairs, designed by Scolari for Giorgetti. The low coffeetable set in front of the sofa is an opium couch purchased from a Venetian antiques dealer.

Second overleaf, right: A corner of the library with a portrait of Massimo Scolari's mother, done by a nephew of Mosé Bianchi, in 1949. The portrait includes elements with symbolic significance: the three roses, and the three pearls on her ring, represent her three sons. Beneath the portrait, a pendulum clock from 1929 and a small mummy of a peregrine falcon, embodying the god Horus, the son of Isis and Osiris, which came from the collection of an early-twentieth-century Egyptologist. In the foreground, a small cherrywood Biedermeier armchair.

Above: In the bathroom, a Turkish sink and an Arabian mirror.

Right: In the bedroom, the *Claudiano* (Claudian) canopy bed, designed by Massimo Scolari for Giorgetti, occupies the center of the room. It has a beechwood structure and the headboard is made of rattan. The hanging night tables are part of the structure of the bed. The walnut armoire dates from the nineteenth century.

" *My basic criterion when I design a space or a design object is flexibility. My home is in a continuous state of transformation and the furnishings need to be able to adapt accordingly.* "

CINI
BOERI

Cini Boeri took a degree at the Politecnico, or Polytechnic University of Milan, in 1951. After working for many years with Marco Zanuso, she began her own professional activity in 1963, taking on civil architecture and industrial design projects. She has designed showrooms (for Venini in Venice, Knoll International in Paris and Milan, and Arflex in Tokyo), villas, apartments, installations of exhibitions, banks, hotels, and the airport of Verona. As an industrial designer, she has worked with Arflex, Artemide, Molteni, ICF, Tronconi, Valli & Valli, Venini, Knoll International, and Rosenthal. Museums throughout the world hold objects designed by Boeri in their collections. Boeri won the Golden Compass award (1979), Stuttgart Design Prize (1985), Design Auswahl '90 Stuttgart, Medaglia d'oro Premio "Apostolo del design" Milano (2003), Premio Dama d'Argento award at the Poldi Pezzoli Museum, Milan (2006). Her published essays and books include Le dimensioni umane dell'abitazione *(Franco Angeli, 1980), "La dimensione del domestico" in* La casa tra tecniche e sogno *(Franco Angeli, 1988), "Progettista a committente" in* Id., Struttura e percorsi dell'atto progettuale *(CittàStudi, 1991), and* Cini Boeri, architetto e designer, *edited by Cecilia Avogadro (Silvana Editoriale, 2004).*

The apartment of Cini Boeri has a Milanese soul. It overlooks one of the loveliest and most significant churches in Milan: the basilica of Sant'Ambrogio (St. Ambrose), the city's patron saint. The interior also has a very Milanese style; it is a simple space, well designed, with a sober elegance. Her home plays on the nuances of shades of white and beige, softened by a note of color, that of the brick-pink wall-to-wall carpeting based upon the warm hues of the church's façade. Cini Boeri, one of the "masters" of Italian design, has lived in this building for thirty years. "I used to live on the second floor with my three sons, Sandro, Stefano, and Tito. Then they moved out and I moved to the floor above into a smaller apartment, though it is still big for me. Now my grandchildren come to visit me: they say that they can study better here than anywhere else." Despite the fact that she rents the apartment, Cini Boeri has renovated the interior with a great sense of freedom, creating in the living area an open, unified space, formed by separate yet still communicating zones: entrance, living area, dining area, and studio. These spaces are separated only by low bookcases and by beam bookcases, set up high, that punctuate the space. Almost all of the furnishings were designed by Boeri and many pieces of furniture are on wheels, a fundamental element of her design. "Unfortunately, I cannot claim to have invented the wheel, but I can say that I put wheels on many of the items of furniture that I have designed, precisely because of this concept of mobility within the home, in which I believe firmly." Typical elements of her projects are transformable furnishings, sliding walls, and equipment inserted into walls. "My basic criterion when I design a space or a design object is flexibility. My home is in a continuous state of transformation and the furnishings need to be able to adapt accordingly." Simplicity and ease of use are two key phrases in this apartment—"also independence," she adds. "In my houses I always try to create spaces where everyone can have their own privacy, a little freedom, which is a fundamental factor in ensuring a happy coexistence." A theme that is of special importance to her is the psychological relationship between man and his environment. The books on the shelves and coffee tables are not only books about architecture, but also on philosophy and politics; Cini Boeri has an inquiring mind and is an inveterate reader.

Opening pages, left: Cini Boeri at her desk in her studio, which is an integral part of the living room. It is divided from the dining room by a low bookcase that she designed for Arflex in 1969, composed of three sections mounted on wheels that can be moved easily and used with the sections in a line, or set at right angles.

Opening pages, right: On the writing desk, a lamp by Jasper Morrison for Flos, *Gio-Ball*; the armchair is from the *Aluminum Group* by Charles and Ray Eames for Vitra, 1958.

Preceding pages: The living area is an open space in which various zones are separated by low bookcases and overhead beam bookcases. The windows frame an enchanting corner of the oldest part of Milan, with the Basilica of Sant'Ambrogio (St. Ambrose). In the foreground is an armchair designed by Charles and Ray Eames.

Opposite and above: A corner of the living room filled with books and photographs. The office chair is by Charles and Ray Eames for Vitra and the two Mies van der Rohe *Barcelona Chairs* are covered with white *capitonné* leather.

The corner studio area is an integral part of the living room, separated from the dining room only by a bookcase on wheels designed for Arflex, in 1969. The architect Boeri uses this little "oasis" to gather her thoughts and to write. For her real work, she has a large professional studio, a short walk from her home, "but at a different address, because I need to separate my work from my private life, to pull out the plug and go back home to relax."

She is surrounded by a sequence of large photographs of her six grandchildren, whom she adores. And also by objects and photographs linked to her history and her family, both of which play a fundamental role in her life; she is a beautiful, elegant, relaxed grandmother. She has always been in touch with young people and she drew the inspiration for certain objects from her children, "because we grew up together," she says. Many other photographs are on the walls, one of Che Guevara, an artist's proof by Joseph Beuys, for whom she has a genuine passion. "I like Beuys's face. I have read his writings, I have seen his artworks. It is difficult to explain precisely because it is a passion." On the walls are sketches and drawings by Giacometti, Duchamp, and

Picasso, but also lots of photographs of her beloved vacation home, built on the island of the Maddalena in the sixties, nicknamed the bunker because of its squared-off shape, "a sort of dark meteorite that fell out of the sky, a stone among the stones of the island."

When she took a degree in architecture at the Politecnico, or Polytechnic University of Milan, in 1951, Cini Boeri already had her first son, Sandro, who was two months old. "He was waiting for me in his baby carriage outside the Politecnico, while I was defending my thesis." Then she worked in the studio of Gio Ponti and for twelve years in the studio of Marco Zanuso; in 1963 she opened her own studio. She has not stopped since then, she has designed villas, apartments, and office buildings; she has designed sofas, lamps, drinking glasses, suitcases, bookcases, and doors, objects that have marked the history of design. Behind her she has more than fifty years of successful architectural and design projects. A rationalist by training, she has always respected the parallel requirements of form and function, conjugating them in step with the times, even far ahead of the times. "As long as I am alive, if I need to design a chair, I need to think

that it has to hold up, that it has to bear the weight of a person, that it should be comfortable, that it should be handsome. I need to keep all these elements in mind."

Cini Boeri has always been an innovative industrial designer. The *Strips* sofabed she designed for Arflex in 1971 was revolutionary. In addition to the *Strips* line of products, which received the Golden Compass award in 1978, another polyurethane sofa, unfinished and flexible, dating from 1971, became a cult object: *Serpentone* (Big Snake). This sofa was sold by the yard and was innovative both in terms of its technology and form. Similarly, the production of the *Ghost* armchair, which she designed for FIAM in 1987, out of a single sheet of folded glass, was one of a series of challenges she faced in those years. "Back then, the manufacturers followed us in a certain manner, supporting our research and experimentation. The *Serpentone* was no joke; behind it was a complex process of technological and materials research done by Arflex with Bayer."

In the house, not only are there objects designed by Cini Boeri, but also classics by the great names of the history of design, such as the chairs by Mies van der Rohe for Knoll International and an armchair by Charles and Ray Eames for Vitra. In the living room, among the posters, photographs, and prints, there is a curious black square: it is the fireplace, truly spare in form.

She still dreams of designing an airplane—in part because an airplane would be so useful for getting out of from Milan quickly and reaching a place that is close to nature. A true Milanese, Cini Boeri is always in movement.

Above: The bedroom is also very spare, with a simple bed on wheels and, instead of the headboard, a long shelf with the books and other objects. The style of Cini Boeri is spare and devoid of decoration.
Opposite: The white kitchen, entirely built to the design of the architect Boeri, is straightforward and functional space with pots and pans hanging on hooks. The plain counter has a cabinet base and the stools are high-tech office furniture.

ADELAIDE
ACERBI ASTORI
ANTONIA
ASTORI

Adelaide Acerbi Astori was born in Milan in 1946. She studied set design at the Brera Academy of Fine Arts. She married Enrico Astori and they founded, along with Antonia Astori, Driade, in 1968. She has overseen the image of the company from the very beginning. Among her most significant work has been the coordinated image of the Astori Prefabricated Company. In 1989 she oversaw the graphics of the apparel labels of a few of Krizia's lines. In 1993 she designed the image and identity for the Museo della Moda (Museum of Fashion) in Milan. In 1994 she edited the images for the book Missonologia. Il mondo dei Missoni. *In 1995 she designed the graphics for the book* Krizia. Una storia *and the book* DriadeBook *edited by Fulvio Irace. Since 1983 she has been the art director and the director of graphics of D.E./Driade Edizioni, a magazine of home accouterments for the third millennium. Since 1995 Acerbi Astori has been in charge of communications for the dadriade showrooms in Milan, Berlin, and Tokyo. She has supervised the coordinated image of the Bagatti Valsecchi Museum in Milan since 1994, and the image of the Bernareggi Museum in Bergamo since 1999. She has also overseen, since 2001, the image of the Museum of the Villa Belgiojoso Bonaparte in Milan.*

A married couple of entrepreneurs, Enrico and Adelaide Astori, commissioned the family architect, Antonia Astori, Enrico's sister, to renovate their house in Milan. Together the three of them founded a company in 1968, called Driade, which has an orientation toward working with innovative designers. The first renovation project that Antonia Astori carried out in this apartment in 1976 was almost off-putting—vast, unnaturally green wall-to-wall carpeting, very seventies in style, and quite amusing. It was extensively photographed and published in the magazines of the time. "We were all very young, and home design was very informal. As time went by, our daughters grew up and our needs changed, we ourselves changed, and of course Italy changed. We needed a more impressive house to entertain in, we wanted to entertain on a more serious level, and Antonia did a wonderful interior design project for us, making structural changes as well," Adelaide Acerbi Astori recalls. Signor and Signora Astori loved to surround themselves with artists, industrial designers, and intellectuals. Among their circle of new friends were Philippe Starck, Borek Sipek, and Oscar Tusquets, industrial designers who were blazing trails in

new directions and setting new trends for their company. Moreover, they needed a house that reflected their own twin passions, art and music. "Art is one of my passions because I studied set design at the Academy of Fine Arts of Brera. For me, it is one of the most important things in life, and all of my work springs from a general reference to art," explains Adelaide Acerbi Astori, whose responsibilities in the family corporation involve managing public relations and communications, overseeing photography, and creating a corporate image.

In the apartment there are works by contemporary artists Tadini, Rotella, and Bartolini: "I have this collection because Enrico, in order to make me happy, always gives me artworks for my birthdays. He even had Rotella do my portrait. With these artists, I have a friendship, a human relationship." Her other passion, which she shares with Enrico, is music, especially opera, to such a degree that Adelaide knows some of her favorite operas by heart.

When the house was renovated, in 1988, Enrico and Adelaide had some very specific ideas about how they wanted to partition the space and about the materials they wanted to use. Their

idea was to create a very open home, filled with interpenetrating spaces that were never entirely closed off. It was necessary to expand the living area, and the decision was made to restructure the veranda, turning it into a large dining area.

Antonia accommodated their requests: "For the veranda, for instance, Enrico had said, 'I'd like a veranda like a Viennese café.' I remembered that once when I was in Trieste in a small café I had noticed a number of little tables made of iron, wood, and brass in different shapes, which inspired me to design the three different little café tables made of marble, in different colors, in the *Sans Souci* collection—a collection that was created in this apartment and that consists of a few special pieces of furniture, very carefully made and designed, such as the café tables, the canopy bed, two writing desks, a vertical chest of drawers, and a movable home office, designed not so much with a computer in mind, but rather focusing on memory. It is a collection of both historic memory and artisanship." Antonia Astori's main responsibility is to work on the wall shelving systems. "In that work, I am like a very rigorous engineer, very aware of the aspects of mass production, but every once in a while, maybe two or

three times in my life, I designed a collection that has nothing to do with mass production—an attempt to recover memories. In those cases I like to use traditional materials, without any concern for costs. It is a distraction from my every-day work."

When this small and very refined collection was put into production, with just fifty numbered pieces of each type of furniture, Fulvio Irace named it the *Sans Souci* collection. "He saw Enrico as a latter-day Frederick II, because he likes to gather around himself a little court of eclectic, cultivated individuals, and he said that I had designed a collection a bit as if I had had a castle in mind," explains the designer.

For the accommodation and arrangement of a large number of books, it was necessary to create a neutral structure, a shell that would not interfere with the true protagonists of the house—the furniture and spectacular objects, such as the chairs, vases, carpets, mirrors, sofas, and artworks that populate the stage setting that is the Astori home. Antonia decided to resolve the problem with the *Oikos* modular wall system that she had designed for Driade. "My father was an engineer who made prefabricated structures, and

Antonia Astori was born in Melzo (Milan) in 1940. She took her degree in industrial and visual design at the Athenaeum in Lausanne in 1966. Since 1968 she has been working on design with the Driade company. Many of her designs for furniture systems and single pieces of furniture were conceived as "architecture for a room." The best known is the Oikos system, designed in 1972, which was awarded the Golden Compass in 1981. Alongside her work as a designer, she works as an interior designer, with projects involving homes, offices, shops, and showrooms. She has been working since 1984 with the French fashion designers Marithé and François Girbaud, designing their shops in Paris and around the world. She designed the Bang & Olufsen shop in Munich. She designed the offices and showrooms for the Driade factory in Fossadello di Caorso, as well as the many dadriade shops around the world. Astori has also designed many Driade installations for furniture fairs in Milan, Cologne, and Frankfurt. She is currently preparing, with Enrico and Adelaide Acerbi Astori, a major exhibition on Driade that will open at the Pinakothek der Moderne in Munich in late 2006.

Previous pages, left: The owner of the house, Adelaide Acerbi, wife of Enrico Astori, and the architect, Antonia Astori, responsible for the renovation of the interior design, photographed next to the *Watteau I* vase by Borek Sipek, Driade, 2004.
Previous pages, right: View of the veranda from the entrance. In the foreground, the little *Odette* vase made of porcelain and silver, by Borek Sipek, Driade, 1989.

Above, left: On the veranda, the wall system from the *Sans Souci* line, by Antonia Astori for Driade, houses the *Odette* vase by Borek Sipek and a number of vases by Sipek. On the *Karl* café table by Antonia Astori for Driade is a transparent glass vase by Venini. The *Costes* chairs by Philippe Starck, 1985, are placed around the *Kolo*, *Karine*, and *Karl* café tables designed by Antonia Astori in 1989, all for Driade.
Above: The entrance that opens into the living room is lined with books contained in the modular *Oikos* system, designed by Antonia Astori for Driade. The *Pratone* chair, designed by Giorgio Ceretti, Pietro Derossi, and Riccardo Rosso, in 1966, is produced by Gufram. The painting is by Luciano Bartolini. The small *Red and Blue* armchair by G. T. Rietveld dates from 1918 and was reproduced by Cassina.

I believe that I assimilated an understanding of modular composition from him and transferred it to the field of home furnishings. In the *Oikos* systems, which are mass produced, there is an engineering aspect but it's not an original idea. The architects of the thirties had already explored it all; they were the true pioneers. In the seventies we simply implemented what they had imagined and reproposed their systems, encouraged by a sociological change, when people were more prosperous and had lots more things to store, and houses were being used to the last cubic millimeter." The systems, which are modular and flexible, are articulated in this house to a number of sizes and depths, with bookshelves, display cases, wardrobes, shelves, and containers, in shades of gray or soft pastel colors. "The *Oikos* system underwent an evolution, both in terms of technology and color. At first, in the seventies, it was all white, then in the eighties there was a Japanese influence and I introduced grays, blacks, silk-screened glass, and then more pastel colors. The basic structure remained unchanged; what changed was the skin, which is subject to the variations of fashions and the periods in which we live. The modulation was so vast, with three dif-

ferent depths and four heights, that no new modules were added." The system of wall shelving was used as an organizing tool, increasing the space available for other things.

The protagonist is design. The furnishings are not all by Driade; there is furniture from Cappellini, Poltrona Frau, Gufram, and Cassina. "I think that homes should not be experienced as fixed spaces; they should reflect your entire life, the memories of the trips you take, the emotions you experience, the books you read; this is a home made by an architect, but it is lived in. If I want to move things, I do it, if I want to set the table for five or for thirty people, I can do it. I live in this private space in total liberty." The house in London, a two-story Victorian house where the Astoris have lived for four years, also had a theatrical element in the living room—a fresco on the walls by Vittorio Locatelli based upon a painting by Paolo Uccello. It was a comfortable house with simple and functional furnishings. Enrico Astori let the two masterminds of these interiors speak. He does not offer any comments since he is on one of his many business trips, in China, trying to figure out which way the world is moving.

*" My father was an engineer who
made prefabricated structures,
and I believe that I assimilated an
understanding of modular composition
from him and transferred it
to the field of home furnishings. "*

Preceding pages: In the living room, the parquet
floor is covered by the *La Bruyère* carpet by Linde
Burkhardt, Driade, 1993. The sofa with wheels,
upholstered in white linen, is the *Neoz* by Philippe
Starck, 1997, as are the *Lola Mundo* stools, 1988,
all by Driade. The large *Osmond* mirror by Driade
was designed by Pietro Derossi, in 1993. Around
the *Karine* café table, by Antonia Astori, are *Lucas*
chairs by Oscar Tusquets for Driade, 1991.

Above, left: A blown-glass vase by Venini.
Above, right: The *Astrolabio* (Astrolabe) table
and café tables are by Oscar Tusquets, 1988. The
Florian II vase is by Borek Sipek, as is the daybed
Prosim Sni, while the *Lola Mundo* chair is by Philippe
Starck. The large painting in the background is by
Emilio Tadini.
Opposite: The *Karine* café table with multicolored
marble inlays is by Antonia Astori and forms part
of a series of geometric café tables. The *Wilhelm*
writing desk was designed by Antonia Astori for
the *Sans Souci* collection; on the writing desk is
an artwork by Luciano Bartolini. The Lucas chairs
are by Oscar Tusquets, Driade. Behind the writing
desk extends the *Tolomeo* (Ptolemy) lamp by
Michele De Lucchi for Artemide.

Preceding pages, left: In the display case of the *Oikos* system by Antonia Astori, a collection of drinking glasses and blown-glass vases. On the *Astrolabio* (Astrolabe) table by Oscar Tusquets, 1988, stands the *Florian II* vase by Borek Sipek and an antique fruitstand; the *Lucas* red velvet chairs are by Oscar Tusquets.

Preceding pages, right: A view into the *Driadechef* kitchen, with furnishings designed by Antonia Astori. For the surfaces, a valuable marble was used. The *Sarapis* stools are by Philippe Starck; the dishes and bowls are from the *Victoria* series by Oscar Tusquets: all by Driade. The slender *Diafana* (Diaphanous) hood was designed by Oscar Tusquets for BD Ediciones. The painting on the left is by Edival Ramosa.

Opposite: The bedroom has a *Franz Joseph* canopy bed, by Antonia Astori, Driade, 1989. The *Alma Ditha* makeup table is also by Antonia Astori for the *Sans Souci* collection. In the foreground, a *Jansky* chair by Borek Sipek, Driade, 1987.

Above, left: The bathroom adjoining the bedroom.

Above, right: The bathroom with custom-made furnishings designed by Antonia Astori. The surfaces covering the floors and the walls are made of Carrara marble. In the center of the floor, a black marble inlay forms a decorative motif with the initials of the owners of the house.

" I came to live in this apartment, about ten years ago, when I was beginning to work in Paris for the Maison Christian Dior, and I was highly influenced by the décor of certain French interiors. "

Daniela Puppa took her degree in architecture at the Politecnico, or Polytechnic University, of Milan; most of her career has focused on the fields of industrial design, fashion design, and interior decoration. She began her career as an editor for the magazine Casabella, *and in 1977 assisted in the creation of* Modo. *Her first projects in the field of industrial design involved experimentation with the avant-garde groups Alchimia and Memphis, with exhibitions and events tied to Radical Design. She has designed for FontanaArte, Barovier & Toso, and Valli & Valli. In the field of fashion, she has designed accessories for such international brands as Gianfranco Ferré, Christian Dior, and the LVMH group. In the field of textile design she is a consultant for Poltrona Frau. For the Ratti and Braghenti group, she has designed their creative offices, presentation spaces, and retail spaces. She has been a consultant for retail stores including Metropolis, La Rinascente, Croff, and Habitat. She was director of the department of Fashion Design at the Domus Academy and curently teaches at the Politecnico of Milan, in the Department of Industrial Design and at the I.U.L.M. in Milan.*

If it is true that a home reflects one's passions, the home of the architect and industrial designer Daniela Puppa speaks to us of her love for Japanese culture, for French décor, and for collections of objects on the theme of the sea: seashells, fish, and coral.

Daniela Puppa lives in a large and charming apartment, on the main floor (or *piano nobile*) of an eighteenth-century *palazzo*, in the historic center of Milan. It is a structure that is "special even when empty," with gilded friezes that adorn the arched moldings of the sumptuous doorways; the original parquet has old-fashioned inlay work; and the high, vaulted ceilings feature floral decorations in stucco. In this structure, which is reminiscent of certain Parisian interiors where the rooms open one into another in a spectacular enfilade, Daniela Puppa has succeeded in fusing contemporary design and vintage modern furniture with highly personal references to Asian style. "I came to live in this apartment about ten years ago, when I was beginning to work in Paris for the Maison Christian Dior, and I was highly influenced by the décor of certain French interiors. I wanted, for instance, to emphasize the doors with an element of charm, the color gold,

widely used in France to emphasize architectural details, from the exterior as well: domes and fences." The original plan of the apartment had a purely functional hallway that linked the various rooms: it was eliminated and used to create utility areas, such as the storage room. The architect Puppa preferred to allow the rooms to open one into the other. "It is the home of a single person. The space is open because the rooms all communicate one with the next."

Each room has its walls painted a different color, pink in the living room, light blue in the bedroom, yellow in the kitchen. The doors that connect them have imposing cornices with oculus-transoms above them. And each room is characterized by different decorative themes. In the entrance, which overlooks a large veranda, the atmosphere of a *jardin d'hiver* has been created, with gouaches on the theme of the palm tree, paintings with garden designs, botanical prints, oriental illustrations of the plants she loves best, the palm tree and the banana tree. A genuinely green room: "Since I didn't have a terrace but I did find a veranda, I thought it would be nice to have trees in my home; and what tree could be better suited to this luminous space than a palm

tree, which, however, grows only slowly and with difficulty. This veranda must originally have been a genuine loggia because the arches seem to be French doors." Classical design objects harmonize with contemporary design pieces, and there are some daring combinations, such as the small classical *bergères* (eighteenth-century French armchairs) alongside leopard-spotted chairs from the forties and two wicker armchairs of Scandinavian design from the fifties, by Jacobsen (reproduced by Cappellini). Collections are one of Daniela Puppa's great loves, and she is a tireless "treasure" hunter, browsing the flea markets and *brocantes*. The decorative theme in the living room/studio is seashells and corals, assembled in an antique piece of Japanese furniture or else framed like paintings. The kitchen, on the other hand, has as its decorative theme fish, depicted in antique prints on the walls and in the *noran*, a small Japanese decorative curtain, whose graphic motif is echoed in the doors of the apartment: "I wanted a light filter and these curtains helped to screen the windows but also to emphasize the doors. In Japan, their connotation is that of a shop sign." In the kitchen, a true piece of cult design, is the first item from the Alchimia collec-

tion, the prototype of the table designed by Ettore Sottsass, surrounded by the *Ant* chairs by Arne Jacobsen for Fritz Hansen.

Daniela Puppa has followed an anomalous path as an architect: she began her career as a journalist in the seventies, then continued working as an industrial designer with such avantgarde experimental groups as Alchimia and Memphis. Then she began her adventure in the field of fashion, which began with Gianfranco Ferré, where she designed collections of accessories, and which culminated ten years later when she designed the leather accessories lines for the Maison Christian Dior. "I believe that if a room and a home is a living space for the human body, a purse is the first extension of the body—it is our little portable home. Basically, I have always loved fashion. I have always been curious about materials and finishes: I continued working with Gianfranco Ferré in the adventure with Dior, and then I continued alone, with Dior Uomo, or menswear."

She has designed many objects and lamps: in her house there is an array of spotlights to emphasize the corners. Her lamps for FontanaArte, she tells us, "developed out of the

Opening pages, left: Daniela Puppa next to the standing lamp *Prima Signora* (First Lady), which she designed for FontanaArte, in 1992.
Opening pages, right: A detail of the bedroom, Japanese in inspiration, with a small writing desk built at the foot of the bed.

Preceding pages, left: In her studio, the lamp on the table is the first lamp that Daniela Puppa designed for FontanaArte; it is called the *Plutone* (Pluto). On the Japanese stair is a collection of seashells, corals, exquisite Asian ceramics, and a small lamp by Gio Ponti for FontanaArte. A large seashell is displayed in a picture frame; the small chair is by Oro dei Farlocchi, Milan.
Preceding pages, right: In the living room is the *XL* lamp by Daniela Puppa for FontanaArte. On the wall are drawings with dedications from her friends, the architects Mariscal, De Lucchi, and Sottsass.

Above: The large veranda into which the entrance hall leads is a room as green as a *jardin d'hiver*. The walls are lined with a collection of drawings, prints, and paintings that have a common theme of palm and banana trees. The alabaster lamp was designed by Daniela Puppa for Croff.

Preceding pages, right: The *Mokambo* sofa by Daniela Puppa for Brunati is upholstered in with pink and red striped fabric. Throughout the apartment, there are Chinese carpets with animal motifs. The retro atmosphere is emphasized by the imposing arched door with friezes and moldings made of gilt stucco work.

Opposite: The kitchen has a decorative theme of fish, depicted in antique prints and in the *noran*, a small decorated Japanese curtain hanging on the window. The *Obi* table lamp by Daniela Puppa for FontanaArte takes its inspiration from the Japanese kimono sash; it is a folded ovoid sheet of glass.
Above: The table designed by Ettore Sottsass is a cult object, the first piece designed for the Alchimia collection; the *Ant* chairs are by Arne Jacobsen for Fritz Hansen. On the shelves that run the length of the wall, glass and ceramic objects designed by Daniela Puppa.

pursuit of a feeling, a story." One example is the *Prima Signora* (First Lady) lamp (FontanaArte), inspired by the movie *Raise the Red Lantern*; it is reminiscent of a lantern. Light is the protagonist of the space in her home. "I am interested in the use of light, a very soft style of illumination. My lamps have a shared theme of a diffuse and atmospheric light; they are not strong, powerful, sharp lights."

Throughout the apartment, the leitmotiv is Chinese carpets, graphic and colorful, with figures of animals. Her love for oriental culture, which emerges in many details, developed out of her business travel. "I especially love the Japanese culture, because it blends a great simplicity with a precise range of colors—white, dark blue, and a few shades of brick red. It has a great formal and graphic elegance." She purchased some of her furniture in Japan, such as the classic piece of furniture-qua-staircase: it is usually used to climb up to a loft with a futon, but in her apartment it holds a collection of exquisite oriental ceramics. The other piece of Japanese furniture is not luxurious, very elementary, made of a light-colored wood: a deep wardrobe in which the Japanese store a trousseau. In her bedroom, there

is a Japanese *kami* lamp (*kami* means "paper"). On the table in the kitchen and in the entrance is another lamp inspired by the obi, or kimono sash—a sheet of glass folded and pierced by the wire that forms its base.

The most beautiful house is a house that people live in as a place of total life, where the fundamental elements for the quality of life are your neighbors, your neighborhood, and your environment.

ENZO
MARI

Enzo Mari was born in Novara in 1932. He attended the Brera Academy of Fine Arts, in Milan, and devoted himself to researching "the psychology of vision and design methodology." He chose to work in the field of industrial design as well and has developed more than 1,700 projects for Italian and international manufacturers, including Alessi, Artemide, Danese, Driade, KPM, Olivetti, Zanotta, Magis, Muji, Hida Sangyo, Gebruder Thonet, Zani & Zani, Interflex, Robots, Olivari, Daum, and FIAM. His work has been exhibited in many museums and shows, among them the Venice Biennale, the Milan Triennale, the Schloss Charlottenburg in Berlin, and the M.I.C. (Museo Internazionale delle Ceramiche, or International Ceramics Museum) in Faenza. Examples of his artworks and design creations are present in the permanent collections of numerous archives and museums, including the C.S.A.C. (Centro Studi ed Archivio della Comunicazione, or Center for Studies and Archives of Communications) in Parma, the Galleria Nazionale d'Arte Moderna (National Gallery of Modern Art) in Rome, and the Museum of Modern Art in New York. His exploration and research has brought him more than forty prizes and awards, including four Golden Compass awards.

Enzo Mari says that his real home is the professional studio where he works and spends most of his waking time. "The quality of your life depends to a great degree on the quality of your work," he says, and he is convinced that a home should be experienced as a place of total life. For more than thirty years he has lived—with his wife, Lea Vergine, an art critic and the author of texts on contemporary art—in an apartment that is a sort of green oasis, with its sweet-smelling wisteria and a century-old magnolia tree in the courtyard of an old *palazzo* in the historic center of Milan, where in the nineteenth century Radetsky had his stables. Enzo Mari, the guru of international design, likes to take shelter on his terrace, which he has transformed into a garden where he tends to his grove of bonsai trees. He tells us that he has always loved plants: "When I was young, I was poor, but I wished I could own a forest. Since I could not achieve this dream, I began to cultivate little trees that I found between the trolley tracks, and little buds and sprouts that I found in the city parks. I had to keep them from growing too much, though, because I didn't have much space available. I would trim the roots and keep them in tiny vases. Back then, in the fifties, I knew noth-

ing about bonsai trees. Now I have about a hundred of them, and some of them are more than forty years old."

The Enzo Mari that one discovers between the walls of his home is a surprising individual. Those who are familiar with his rigorous, uncompromising personality tend to identify him with the spartan interior of his studio. It is only after entering his home and seeing the miniature greenery on his terrace that one begins to detect the more sensitive side of his personality. He has lived in Milan for seventy years and lately he has many bad things to say about the city. "When I look at what a monstrosity Milan has become, I realize that the forms of Milan bespeak ignorance and arrogance: there are very few positive examples being set, and that is why people behave so poorly."

He has a studio in his home as well: the apartment has very high ceilings, and Mari has taken advantage of the space above eye level, inventing a catwalk where he has installed a library. The furnishings are spare: the modular plastic bookcase, the *Glifo* (Glyph), manufactured by Gavina in the sixties; a wire table designed for Robots; a beechwood and varnished aluminum rocking chair,

designed recently for Thonet. This studio is a sort of treasure house of wonders, full of odd curiosities. In an old set of post boxes that Mari rescued from a concierge, he has gathered objects of all sorts: notebooks, albums, pencil cases for drafting pencils, maps and charts, postcards, fossils, photographs, and family memorabilia. This collection of disparate objects resembles to some degree the professional studio where Mari has accumulated over the years a great variety of prototypes, curious objects, artworks, models, books, annual collections of magazines, souvenirs, writings, his archives, and papers of every sort. The austere space is intimidating, particularly in the presence of Professor Mari arguing polemically about the world of consumption and asking searching questions about the future of design. "The market requires objects that age rapidly, all objects are manufactured with the idea that they are disposable. We are destroying the world. We have used up almost all our resources." His gaze is serious, his voice urgent. "I have reached the point of renouncing this profession entirely, even though I love the work I do, because the manufacturers ask me to design something in fifteen minutes. What they want from me are inventions, not

designs, not projects. They even go so far as to modify the design with gadgets of all sorts, and then they ask me to put my name on it. When I say that a design is an act of war, it is because what manufacturers care about is selling, not doing the right thing. The entire discourse of design culture is very flatly slaughtered by ignorance and arrogance." Mari is one of very few designers who has about twenty different objects, first designed nearly fifty years ago, still in production.

In the studio, he has the equipment for his work as an artist and an experimenter. But at home, as he chats with his wife and his guests at lunch or dinner, the conversation wanders in other directions, art, nature, and music. Enzo Mari is a curious man, very ironic and self-deprecating in the stories he tells, and almost shy in talking about himself.

"The furnishings of this apartment evolved over time. The first furniture we had were cardboard boxes, leftovers from installations. Now, in our home, what we have for the most part are my objects because they were inexpensive: they are unmanufactured prototypes or items that the manufacturers offered me at a good price. I have

Preceding pages, left: Enzo Mari in his studio.
Preceding pages, right: A wooden object that depicts a hammer and sickle; it was part of a research project carried out in the seventies based on a painting Mari made in 1952. This object was exhibited in a show on religious and political symbols.

Above: The professional studio contains his archives, artworks, objects, souvenirs, and many prototypes.
Opposite: Some of Mari's most famous chairs. From the left: a wooden chair designed thirty years ago, a product of "*autoprogettazione*" (literally, "self-design"); a yellow *Box* chair designed for Anonima Castelli in 1975, made of plastic and metal (it can be completely dismantled); the spare aluminum *Tonietta*, with a leather upholstered seat, Zanotta, 1985 (Golden Compass, 1987). The lamp is part of the *Aggregato* (Aggregate) system designed by Mari for Artemide, in 1974.

Overleaf: A number of rooms in the studio are set aside as artisanal workshops, with a small carpenter's table, a vise, and all of the equipment needed to make scale models using wood and other materials. The space is brimming with papers and prototypes.

Opposite: Mari redesigned this luminous space and created a balcony with bookcases. The yellow chair on the left is *Box*. The metal table to the right of the doorway was designed by Mari for Robots.
Above: The leather upholstered armchair is the *Sanluca*, designed by Achille and Piergiacomo Castiglioni. Next to it is a floor lamp from the *Aggregato* (Aggregate) series, designed by Mari for Artemide in 1974.
Above, right: An old set of post boxes, taken from a concierge, is used as a container for a vast assortment of objects. The modular plastic *Glifo* (Glyph) bookcase was produced by Gavina in the sixties.

chosen not to hang a lot of paintings on the walls, because I think a painting is like a book—you don't keep all your books open in your library. If there are any paintings by me, it is only because I didn't know where else to put them."

In the living room, there is a strange fireplace that looks like a totem of some sort. Mari designed and built it himself. "The fireplace comes from my memories, from the house I lived in when I was a child. I wanted an apartment that had a fireplace, but I couldn't find one. So I purchased a prefabricated fireplace and put it in with the help of a bricklayer and then covered it up like this out of a sense of play, it is a decorative object." On the various mantels, there are a photograph of his daughter, antique tiles, drawings, and stones. Near the fireplace, is the historic chair designed in 1934 by Gerrit T. Rietveld, made of unfinished elmwood with exposed bolts. The two sofas are also informal; one is a prototype that was never put into production, the other is the *Daynight* sofabed, designed by Mari. On top a *Glifo* modular bookcase are "programmed" artworks from the sixties, the result of aesthetic research that Mari did on the perception of three-dimensional space

In a career spanning more than forty years as a designer, Mari has never ceased to wonder about the significance of design and art. He has always emphasized the contradictions of a socially oriented profession in a capitalistic and consumerist society. "I have always been trying to produce different behavioral models, hoping that they might be able to influence the culture of individuals. The real potential of a design lies in its capacity to modify the way people behave and act," he declares. He has never given in to the blandishments of easy commercial success, and research has been the cornerstone of his designs: the children's toys he designed for Danese in the sixties; the *Tappeto Volante* (Flying Carpet) bed for Interflex, which became exceedingly famous for the cherubs by Raphael on the headboard; his lamps, the chairs with girls' names *Tonietta* (which won the Golden Compass in 1987), *Delfina*, and *Paolina*; lamps for Artemide; the table *Legato* for Driade (which won the Golden Compass in 2001), and many other objects that have become popular around the world.

With a personality that makes him willing to subject anything and everything to discussion, Enzo Mari criticizes the world of consumption,

Left: Displayed at the entrance to the studio is an inflatable figure from Munch's The Scream and a wooden sculpture based on Mari's formal experimentations.

Opposite: On a modular Glifo bookcase are "programmed" artworks from the sixties, the fruit of an aesthetic research project Mari did on the perception of three-dimensional space. Among them is a model for the allegory "Eppur si muove," designed by Mari for the Sixteenth Milan Triennale in 1979, with the words "*Rivoluzione-Restaurazione*" (Revolution-Restoration); the *Polluce* (Pollux) lamp, designed for Artemide in 1963; and spherical ceramic pieces by Luigi Mainolfi.

Overleaf, left: In the living room, Mari has designed an unusual fireplace. On the various shelves of the mantel piece are photographs of Mari with his daughter and antique tiles, letters and numbers.

Overleaf, right: Corners of the entrance to Mari's home with a staircase that leads up to the loft-balcony with its large bookcase. The cylindrical standing vase from the sixties forms part of the *Vasi camicia* (Shirt Vases) collection, designed by Mari for Danese. The artwork in cardboard hanging above the standing vase is by the artist Hidetoshi Nagasawa.

but he is also willing to discuss and question himself and his own work. "If I were asked to give a definition of what I now consider a good designer to be, I would say that he would be like an old farmer who, at the end of his life, decides to plant a grove of chestnut trees. He will not live to eat any of the chestnuts, nor will he be able to rest under the broad spreading branches, nor will he be able to use any of the wood, but he plants it with his grandchildren in mind, at a time when everyone else is cutting down forests and destroying nature. And that is the model I set out for myself."

Mari doesn't believe that houses should be designed by architects alone. He believes that whoever designs a house should also be a psychologist. "The most beautiful house is a house that people live in as a place of total life, where the fundamental elements for the quality of life are your neighbors, your neighborhood, and your environment." In his home, design is present in a discreet manner, because Mari believes that "the quality of living should not depend only upon the quality of a few objects, but also upon many other elements that make up a house: music, books, artworks, light, and a nice garden."

MARCO
ZANUSO JR.

Marco Zanuso Jr. was born in Milan in 1954 and took his university degree in Florence in 1978. He spent time in the United States, where he became familiar with Land Art and looked into the new experiments being done with solar energy. Upon his return to Europe, he worked on a landscape architecture project in the Rastlos area of Vienna. From 1979 on, he worked in the studio of Marco Zanuso Sr. and began teaching at the Politecnico, or Polytechnic University, of Milan. He then worked with Enzo Mari and Achille Castiglioni, great masters of Milanese industrial design. In 1980 he opened his own studio in Milan. Since 1991 he has been in partnership with Daniele Nava and works on interior decoration for offices and private residences. Among his projects in architecture, the Piccolo Teatro in Milan (with Marco Zanuso Sr.), on which he worked from 1978 until 1996, the Teatro Carlo Fossati and the Auditorium Mondadori in Segrate. Between 2001 and 2004 he was in charge of the corporate image of the Supermercati GS (with Daniele Nava). He is a contributing industrial designer for Cappellini, Driade, De Padova, and FontanaArte.

He is the nephew of the great Marco Zanuso, one of the masters of Italian design, and he too chose the profession of architect and industrial designer. In order to distinguish himself from his famous uncle, he added a "Jr." to his name. "I chose architecture in part because of the influence of my uncle. I believe that if it is done with passion, it is an excellent cultural school, a nice blend of different schools of knowledge. Then, whether you can make a living with it or not is another matter, but that is true for just about all the liberal arts degrees. If I had to choose again now, I think I would focus on leaving Italy, and then I would decide whether and what to study." Together he and his uncle worked for many years on the design of the Piccolo Teatro and the design of the Teatro Fossati in Milan. "My uncle taught me a certain rigor. He taught me to try to really understand what we are trying to do and why, and then to try to do things well, by the standards of the profession: what emerges is an equilibrium made up of elegance and creativity." Zanuso Jr. has a passionate love of design and he has designed many objects and pieces of furniture for the leading Italian manufacturers: Memphis, Driade, De Padova, Cappellini, Carlo Moretti, and

FontanaArte. He says that the project that he loves best was his *Cleopatra* café table, made by Memphis: "They did such a good job!" But he has also renovated public buildings, private homes, and recently—with his partner, Daniele Nava—he redesigned the interior image of the GS supermarket chain: over two hundred points of sale in all Italy. "The objective was to create inside a supermarket a number of corners that would make it resemble a genuine market: a little square for fruit and vegetables, the shops of the butcher, the baker, the fish vendor."

Marco Zanuso Jr. has been living, for the past two years, with his wife, Marzia, in this apartment with a fairly traditional structure, in the heart of Brera, in Milan. He had always liked the place; he knew it already because a friend of his lived there. The building had originally been a factory, then it was converted into an apartment building. It has preserved a certain character, with spacious rooms, high ceilings, and a fine old-fashioned parquet floor. But in particular Zanuso had fallen in love with the light. The apartment has extraordinary light. When he renovated it, he moved the kitchen so that it opened onto the living room: "I like to be in the kitchen

and communicate with the people in the living room." Then he oversaw a series of details, colors and furnishings that give the apartment a warm and straightforward character. The space is expansive and the furnishings are reduced to the bare minimum, making it seem even more spacious: there are no knickknacks, nothing superfluous. Order is a primary necessity, at least for him. He needs to have an orderly relationship among things: "The space between objects is important. Space without a sense of equilibrium can create a profound malaise." The furniture and the bookcases in the hallway were designed and custom built; otherwise, all the furniture comes from their previous homes. His design projects are present in the apartment, though not all of them. "Often, my projects spring from a personal need. I think of something that is missing in the environment that surrounds me: I designed the television carts and the computer dollies for myself before designing them for De Padova." He likes color and considers it a tool for modifying space, making it more personal. "Color per se is abstract, but in a home it serves to give a certain weight to the entire system. In this apartment there is a lot of red—many

different reds and many shades of white and cream and beige." In the living room the spot of color is the red of a famous armchair, the *Vanity Fair* by Poltrona Frau: "It is a very beautiful object. It is the idea of an armchair as a child might draw it. I like its enveloping physicality, and it is also incredibly heavy!"

There is design in the dining area, too, with a large square table by De Padova, which also becomes a table for writing, studying, and sketching. And he could hardly have left out the chairs by Arne Jacobsen for Fritz Hansen: an evergreen classic of Scandinavian design. Likewise for the hanging lamp above the table, by Poulsen. "Nordic design is not arrogant, and it gives me a sense of social interaction that is sensual and civil at the same time."

Zanuso Jr. has designed many lamps: one of these lamps for FontanaArte was inspired by the old-fashioned branching candelabra, but it is a highly technological object because he likes to do materials research and to experiment. "For an entire series of lamps I used borosilicate glass, in the form of tubes of varying diameters, the tubes that are used for test tubes in chemistry. It is a thin and transparent glass that nevertheless with-

Preceding pages, left: Marco Zanuso Jr. sitting at a table produced by De Padova; the *Ant* chairs are by Arne Jacobsen for Fritz Hansen. The lamp hanging over the table is the *PH5* by Poul Henningson, Poulsen, 1957. Set on the low bookcase is a *Minimal 5* lamp, in borosilicate glass, by Zanuso Jr., for FontanaArte, 2004. The large painting is by Miguel Laporta.
Preceding pages, right: A view of the kitchen.

Above and opposite: The living room is large and luminous. The protagonist, at the center of the room, is the red leather *Vanity Fair* armchair. The pair of Piedmontese tortile columns from the seventeenth century are family heirlooms. Between the windows, a drawing by Ettore Sottsass.
Opposite: The round table in the foreground, which can be adjusted in height, is by Santa & Cole, 1979. The café table next to the red armchair is from the *Shaker* collection by De Padova.

Opposite: The white sofa made by an upholsterer echoes the classic design of the English club sofa. The painting above the sofa is by Nathalie du Pasquier.
Left: The bedroom as seen from the corridor.

Overleaf, left: The bedroom with the bed by Konstantin Grcic for Driade; a standing lamp with a large shade, *PO/9909*, designed by Marco Zanuso Jr. for Cappellini; a number of antiques, including a *bergère*, two small armchairs, and a family chest of drawers.
Overleaf, right: The kitchen is very simple, with a working surface under the window, a retro table with a marble top, and old wooden chairs. The furniture was designed by the architect Marco Zanuso Jr., partly in beechwood, and it is partly lacquered. The hanging lamp is the *Aggregato* (Aggregate) series, designed by Enzo Mari.

stands high temperatures very successfully. I use it to create light, evanescent lamps." With another highly resistant material, glass fibers, Zanuso Jr. designs chairs and tables, as well as office chairs for the Arte company. He explains that glass fiber is a material similar to plastic but much stronger and also more expensive. His research into technological materials continues: he has presented at the Salone del Mobile in Milan his *Policromi* (Polychromes) collection, one-offs and numbered editions, produced by La Galérie Italienne of Paris, entirely based on the automatized processing of sheet steel and sheet aluminum, which is cut with a laser and folded in a manner reminiscent of Japanese origami.

He says that he cannot stand spaces that are too full or cluttered and that he does not love decorations. But he certainly loves art: on the walls—and in some cases still waiting to be hung—are canvases of informal art. "I brought paintings by Miguel Laporta from my house in Barcelona. I especially like contemporary informal art. At times it really strikes me as amusing. It makes me think. Then, occasionally, it is pure magic, an emotion, poetry: I think that the role of art in society is fundamental."

ANTONIO
ANNICHIARICO

*" It's all written plainly on the spot: all you need
to do is read clearly, know how to listen,
and then the design takes form. "*

*Antonio Annichiarico was born in 1953 in Grottaglie,
in Apulia (Puglia). He comes from a family of artisans,
smiths, and ceramists. After earning a degree in
engineering in Bari, in 1977, he decided to devote
himself to the study of architecture and perfect the
art of working in ceramics. As far back as 1979,
he was building and restoring homes in Italy and
elsewhere. In 1985 he was a participant in the
Biennale of Architecture in Venice, with a project
executed entirely in ceramics. In 1988 he oversaw the
set design of Roberto Benigni's first movie Il piccolo
diavolo. For many years, he has been working as an
industrial designer with major corporations such as
Bardelli, Giorgetti, Rapsel, Accademia, Artemide,
Driade, Gabbianelli, and Quattrifoglio. In 1996 he
designed the Città della Musica in Naples, a giant
discotheque. In 1997 he presented at the Galleria
delle Piane in Milan La casa nomade, a collection of
carpets, furniture, and tapestries in ceramics. Since
1988 he has been working with the Teatro Valdoca
of Cesena. He has done interior design and industrial
design projects in Scotland, Morocco, France, and
Japan. In 2006 he designed an unusual collection of
fashion items entitled Rifiuto Speciale (Special
Refuse)—inspired by garbage—as a protest against
the enlargement of a dump in Grottaglie.*

The place where Antonio Annichiarico, architect,
industrial designer, and set designer, has decided
to live is charged with significance. His *masseria*,
or farmhouse, is located in the Apulian countryside, just a few miles from the beach and close to
Martina Franca. It has a meaningful name: *La
Mutata* (The Changeover). The name derives from
its original use, in bygone centuries: it was a sta-
tion for changing horses—a process known in
Italian as *la mutata*—along a major artery linking
the towns of Brindisi and Taranto. The building
has a long history: in the year 1000, it was a
monastery inhabited by Byzantine monks of the
Basilian order; fleeing persecution, they sought
refuge in Apulia and built a monastery on a
piece of land owned by the bishop of Taranto. In
the eighteenth century, it became a hunting
lodge for the bishop of Taranto, a feudal
landowner who was also the Baron of Grottaglie.
Surrounding it, back then, were a thousand
hectares (2,500 acres) of centuries-old forests.
From the nineteenth century on it was used as a
masseria, inhabited by the farmers who tilled and
worked the lands all around in the immense
estate of San Vittore. The *masserie* were once the
residences of the great Apulian landowners;

today they are often renovated and used as vacation resorts or beauty farms.

That was certainly not what Antonio
Annichiarico had in mind when he restored the
building to its original beauty, with a time-
consuming and painstaking renovation project,
transforming it into a house-qua-studio, practically a hermitage, where there is an atmosphere
that conveys a sense of time having stood still. "A
restoration project the way I like to do it, where
there is nothing added, nothing invented that
wasn't already there. It's all written plainly on the
spot: all you need to do is read clearly, know how
to listen, and then the design takes form. I always
begin with my feelings and emotions in my
designs. In my family, everyone was an artisan,
blacksmiths and ceramists, and I inherited a love
for manipulating materials. I move from frescoes
to mosaics. I believe that I am an architect like
those of the Renaissance, who were also artists
and sculptors." Antonio Annichiarico, an authen-
tic Apulian, born in Grottaglie, worked in Milan
for many of the leading companies of the "made
in Italy," as Italians describe "Italian style," including Driade, Artemide, Acerbis, Giorgetti, and
Bardelli, but in 1997 he decided to spend more

time in the land of his birth. "It was partly because I work in ceramics, and this is a center for ceramics production. In Milan, I was a very active industrial designer, at one point thirty-five objects I had designed were all put into production at the same time. But then you realize that there are more important things than the Salon del Mobile, or furniture fairs, social life, exhibitions; you begin to see that it all leaves you with nothing, that what really matters in life is quite different: silence, working with materials, calmly and with serenity, knowing how to listen, being able to spend time in a place that feels right." Annichiarico's house is a place of some allure, a place of the soul that invites one to reflection, but also a space full of signs of vitality and energy, reflective of his sunny nature and Apulian roots. The key words of his philosophy of design are feelings and joy, understood as an internal sense of well-being.

The building is protected by a one-kilometer-long dry-laid stone wall. Between the enclosure wall and the house is a luxuriant garden, crowded with highly scented plants of the Mediterranean vegetation: roses, pomegranate trees, an olive grove and a citrus grove, caper tree and mulberry

trees. The interior is as stark and ascetic as the interior of a monastery. The space is spare, furnished with only a few essential items, all pieces of furniture designed by the master of the house. On the ground floor, a huge hall, with a vaulted ceiling and floors made of a local stone, welcomes the visitor: the only elements of furnishing are a gaming table and a handsome tufa-stone fireplace. On the second floor are the rooms that long ago formed the bishop's apartment: they radiate around a central patio—an internal courtyard that remains sheltered and cool in the summer, "where the true master is a white dove." Here, the simple tables in steel and the benches made of straw and steel, from the *Santa Sofia* line designed by Antonio Annichiarico, harmonize perfectly with the chianche, or large local rough-hewn stones of the original structure. "I like voids. I like to play with an absence that is often more exquisite and more powerful in emotional terms than any other presence could be. Our spaces are so full—our physical spaces, but our mental spaces as well—that silence is fundamental: this void exalts and emphasizes the architecture, which is usually overwhelmed by the accumulation of things."

Preceding pages, left: Antonio Annichiarico sitting on the steps of the stone staircase that leads to the upper story of the house.
Preceding pages, right: The main entrance gate.

Above: The venerable Apulian *masseria La Mutata*, between Brindisi and Taranto, was restored while preserving its original structure.
Opposite: The interior courtyard of the *masseria*, overlooked by the rooms of the old bishop's apartment, is furnished with tables made of stainless steel, paired with stools made of straw and stainless steel, *Santa Sofia*, designed by Annichiarico.

Overleaf, left: The rooms on the second story radiate around a patio where the floor, made of local stone, is sprinkled with rose and bougainvillea petals. The throne with a straw seat and ceramic backrest was once part of the set design of *Riassunto del Paradiso*, designed by Annichiarico for the Teatro Valdoca.
Overleaf, right: In one of the rooms Annichiarico has set a pattern of ceramic fragments in a cement floor to create a "prayer rug."

" *I like voids. I like to play with an absence that is often more exquisite and more powerful in emotional terms than any other presence could be.* "

The special floors in the rooms were all made by Annichiarico with his own hands. He set colorful ceramic fragments in a layer of white cement, and designed exquisite mosaic "prayer rugs" with an astonishing decorative effect. "For me, a carpet is a great symbol of strength, salvation, and resourcefulness. It reflects man's strength in the face of the adversities of nature. The nomads in the desert had only sand, wind, a camel, and an assortment of colorful roots of wild plants. They dyed the camel hairs, they wove them, and they created carpets that allowed them to survive."

The use of such elementary materials as iron, steel, and wood is one of the principles that guides the design of Annichiarico, who believes that he must respect the *genius loci*, or spirit of the place, with its history and stratifications. A few stage props designed by Annichiarico form part of the furnishings: the throne with its ceramic backrest and the straw chair from the set of *Riassunto del Paradiso*, which he designed for the Teatro Valdoca in Cesena, where Annichiarico has been a regular stage designer since 1988.

In the dining room, there are simple tables made of stainless steel, illuminated by a blend of ceramic and aluminum lamps: they were all

designed by Annichiarico for the collection *La casa nomade* (The Nomadic House), presented at the Galleria Delle Piane in Milan, in 1997: the design of the *La casa nomade* was based on the concept of the carpet. "It is strange how objects might have been conceived at different times and in different places—one in Scotland, one at the Salone del Mobile, or furniture fair, in Milan, one for the Teatro Valdoca—and yet when they are all put together they seem to have been designed for that space. When they are together they find a life of their own because the thought and the emotions that engendered them were the same."

Years ago, Annichiarico designed all the furnishings for the chapel of the Scottish castle of Lord Bute-Stuart on the island of Bute. A chair and kneeling-stool that were part of that project are in the bedroom along with a spear made of ceramics and steel from the installation *Natività* (Nativity), curated by Annichiarico in Lecce, in 2001, at the church of Santa Maria di Cerrate. The common origin of these objects is one and one alone: the thoughts and feelings of an exceptional individual who calls himself "a turncoat engineer, a great rationalist who has experienced the salvation of the instincts."

Above, left: The "prayer rug."
Above, middle: The rooms open one into the next.
Above, right: The dining room, almost monastic in design, with a simple table.
Opposite: The dining room seen from another point of view. The long table in stainless steel and wood is actually three tables side by side; the hanging lamps, made of a combination of ceramics and aluminum, and the ceramic place settings are from the collection *La casa nomade* and were all designed by Annichiarico.

Overleaf left: In front of the sumptuous fireplace, beneath the old archways, a corner of the living room with two ample armchairs.
Overleaf right: One of the bedrooms is nearly free of decoration. The protagonist is the structure of the *masseria* with its large arches and stone floors. The spear made of ceramics and steel came from Annichiarico's *Natività* installation at the church of Santa Maria di Cerrate in Lecce.

FABIO
NOVEMBRE

Fabio Novembre was born in Lecce in 1966 and took his degree in architecture in Milan in 1992. Just two years after his degree, while he was taking a course in film directing in New York, he was hired by Anna Molinari to design the Blumarine store in Hong Kong. He designed other Blumarine stores in London, Singapore, and Taipei. His specialty is designing public spaces: restaurants, discotheques, hotels, shops and stores, and showrooms. He has worked in this field in Milan, New York, and Barcelona. Among his various projects are the Café Atlantique, the restaurant Café Shu, the discotheque Divina in Milan, and the Vittoria Hotel in Florence. He is currently designing the Milanese showroom of Meltin' Pot and shops in Rome and Milan for the American shoe brand, Stuart Weitzman. He has had a major collaboration with Bisazza, a leading corporation in the production of glass mosaic tiles for floors and walls; for them, he designed showrooms in Berlin and New York. In the field of industrial design, he has designed items for Cappellini and for Meritalia, where he is art director.

It all began with a black-and-white photograph by Tazio Secchiaroli, depicting Federico Fellini as he leapt fiercely with a whip on a film set, demonstrating a scene for Marcello Mastroianni. This was the first serious acquisition by a very young Fabio Novembre, who invested in that photograph a considerable portion of the money that he had earned with his first major commission, the design of the Blumarine store in Hong Kong. This choice says a great deal about Fabio's nature: he works on instinct and is passionate. He has that photograph framed in his studio. It has a great symbolic value for him; he has always been in love with the movies, especially the films of Fellini, and he also dreams of resembling Mastroianni.

He has lived in Milan since he left his home town of Lecce at the age of eighteen to study at the Politecnico, or Polytechnic University, of Milan. After graduating, he left Milan to go to New York: "In Milan I became a man: Milan is a network of relationships. It is an emotional welter because, whenever I walk through Milan, I link corners and streets to emotions and feelings, but Milan is everything but an underground place. In New York, everyone has a dream to achieve and anyone can dream of succeeding."

A recent graduate with a degree in architecture, he was in New York, taking a course in film directing, when he was hired by Anna Molinari to design her store in China. Novembre launched himself body and soul into the project, and it was so successful that he was commissioned to do other Blumarine stores in London, Taipei, and Singapore. From that point on, his career climbed steadily. He designed objects for Cappellini, for Meritalia (where he is art director), the Bisazza showrooms in Berlin and New York, a restaurant, a café, a hotel in Florence, and a discotheque in Milan. They are fluid and almost dematerialized spaces in which the perception of space is almost eliminated. Is he an artist or a designer? He replies: "I cannot draw a clear line separating art from music and architecture: they are merely different forms of communication. What interests me is the message."

His first true home, however, had to be in Milan: "I feel very Italian because Italy is a country that seeks out powerful icons: Ferrari, spaghetti with tomato sauce, a slice of salami. And the images of my work please people, too, because they are powerful icons that you remember immediately. I'm not a person who focuses on

Preceding pages, left: Fabio Novembre in his studio, seated on the *And* seating system, in a tricolor version, designed for Cappellini in 2001. Next to his him is his faithful cat, Zip.
Preceding pages, right: The *And* seats from another point of view.

Right: On the third floor, the bedroom of Fabio and Candela. The headboard of the bed—a simple bed frame mounted on wheels—is a large antique mirror. The bedside tables are unusual: the one near the door has a modular piece by Tom Dixon, *Jack*, as its base and a sheet of glass serves as a tabletop. The veiled head lamps are pieces by Corrado Levi, *Edipo* (Oedipus), 2003. The "Love" table on the right, by Robert Indiana, is made of wood. The curious heart-shaped red armchair is from the *Spring Collection* by Ron Arad for Moroso, 1991. The terrace is covered with mosaic tiles from Bisazza.

details." For instance, when he wrote a book about Memphis, he had himself photographed nude by Fabrizio Ruffo: "Nude, because all I had to clothe myself were my theories."

"As soon as I could put together a little money, I rented an industrial shed where they used to make airplanes, in an industrial neighborhood: Via Mecenate, in 1995, was a neighborhood for pioneers, there was nothing there. That industrial shed was a symbolic site. I associated it with the idea of flight. I wanted space, the one true luxury for someone who works with space. It was a perfect moment in my life, and that was when I designed the *And* sofa for Cappellini, an infinite modular item." Giulio Cappellini was a decisive figure for Fabio, and Fabio is very close to him. "Giulio invented everyone—Tom Dixon, Jasper Morrison, the Bouroullec brothers, everyone. He pulled them all out of his top hat. He played the same role that Dino Gavina did in the fifties and sixties: a forerunner."

His new house is an icon as well, a message to be communicated. The house is a metaphor for the Garden of Eden with the recurring symbol of the primordial serpent and constant references to Adam and Eve, the tree of knowledge, and the

apple of temptation. Fabio has found his Eve. She is beautiful. Her name is Candela, and she is Argentine. She bore him a daughter, Verde, and he married her in Las Vegas. "I always knew that she was the story of my life," says Fabio, and tells the story of how he found this space years ago, just when Candela left him, but he chased after her for a year. They got back together following a Salone del Mobile, when he had designed the *S.O.S.* sofa for Cappellini: it is an abbreviation for "Sofa of Solitude" and she heard his cry for help.

The first night that he slept in this house was when Candela and Verde came home from the hospital. "And so, symbolically, we all three slept here for the first time." Dates are always important, especially palindromic dates; Novembre purchased the house on 20/11/02 (the 20th of November, 2002, European style) and was married on 30/11/03 (the 30th of November, 2003).

He explains that, in his youth, he was an altar boy in his church and that—like all former altar boys—he has become a "priest hater," but there is still some sliver of Christianity deep in his soul. Once, he even had himself photographed with a crown on his head, like the Messiah, but instead of thorns, the crown was made of fiber optics:

"Be your own Messiah." In short: "You need to account to yourself. You alone are responsible for your own salvation, so free yourself from your sense of guilt."

When he decided to build himself a home, he identified with Adam and transformed the architecture ideally into a tree: "The tree that cost the real Adam paradise," he says. "I wanted to redeem the serpent, which in the Judeo-Christian tradition is temptation—it offers the fruit to Eve—but in the Buddhist tradition is protection. When Siddhartha ventures into the forest, the animal that aids him when he falls into meditation is a large serpent that rears up over his head to protect him." In the same way, the serpent that protects Fabio and his home is depicted in a significant artwork by Sandro Chia in the mosaic decoration of the ceiling of the kitchen. It is no accident, in fact, that the serpent looms over the desk where Fabio works: it is made of iron, and he made it with his friend Tom Dixon for an Anna Molinari shop in London: "It was my second project. For this twofold symbol of temptation and protection, it was significant to me that a wedding gown should be linked to the image of a serpent. The long and sinuous body of the serpent

Above, from left: At the center of the bedroom there is a bathtub made of cast iron, enameled white. The chest of drawers is by the artist Maarten Baas and above it is a photograph of Fabio and Candela, *Family Portrait*. The spectacular staircase made with heavy slabs of glass makes the space transparent. A red handrail like a heart-shaped ribbon, designed by Fabio Novembre, runs along the staircase. The large methacrylate lamp, *Chandelier*, by Jacopo Foggini, lights the staircase with a thousand red nuances, illuminated by the open shower lined with mosaic gold-leaf tiles by Bisazza.
Opposite: A detail of the staircase with the red heart-shaped handrail and the boiserie wall made of charred wood, by Maarten Baas.

Opposite: The protagonist of the living room is a boiserie of charred wood, by Maarten Baas. The *Org* café tables, made by Cappellini in 2000, were designed by Novembre; the Varadero sofas produced by Meritalia were upholstered by Novembre with a camouflaged fabric. The floor lamp made of wrought iron and crystal is by Duilio Forte.

Above: A silk-screened corner mirror designed by Fabio Novembre, who self-produced it.

Above, right: Above the fireplace, an engraved French shield from 1866 depicting *The Expulsion from the Garden of Eden*. In front of the fireplace, a skylight makes it possible to see and to illuminate the kitchen, below.

Overleaf: Two views of the kitchen. The entire ceiling is covered with Bisazza mosaic tile, with a spectacular artwork by Sandro Chia, depicting the biblical serpent. The lamp made with fragments of crystal is the work of Deborah Thomas. The large countertop in the kitchen, built to plans by Novembre, was produced by Boffi Italia. The large Corian table is etched and backlit from the interior: it features luminous Islamic decorations inspired by the Alhambra. The chairs are by Atelier Van Lieshout. The walls are decorated with plaster stuccoes with a floral motif.

was a bar that was meant to serve as a hanger for a line of wedding gowns, but as soon as they set it up, it seemed too powerful, and they removed it from the store. So I kept the head and put it in my studio."

The house extends over three stories: on the exterior is a pillar, a symbol of the trunk of the tree in the Garden of Eden—Fabio has romantically inscribed it with a heart in white gold mosaic tiles, with the initials "F.C.," for Fabio and Candela. Next to the pillar is a real tree, the Judas tree that always blossoms with pink blooms in the spring.

Following a philosophy all his own, Fabio wanted to created a kitchen space that seemed almost like a dance floor, with plenty of lights and theatrical effects, and a countertop that seemed like a DJ's turntable. "Of course, I like to think about dinner, everyone eating together, as if it were a big collective ritual: and so the table that I designed seats thirteen. And then I like to think of a 'DJ-chef' at the stove, creating the atmosphere of a discotheque."

In the living room on the second floor, the "charred" wooden boiserie, a creation of the Dutch artist Maarten Baas, has a symbolic signifi-

cance: the fire of the fireplace has burned the wood, purifying the boiserie from any and all bourgeois significance. There is another recurring symbolic element in the house, in the form of transparency, which corresponds to nudity. In the stairwell, the steps are made of thick slabs of glass; the shower at the top of the staircase is like a transparent vitrine in gold mosaic tile, and it illuminates the staircase. A red heart-shaped handrail runs the length of the staircase while from the ceiling there hangs a spectacular lamp in shades of red—as if it were a path of constant temptation between love and eros.

Fabio moves between his studio and his home, holding his daughter, Verde, just over a year old, in his arms: he cuddles her and never leaves her alone for a moment. He speaks on the phone, with a black cat sleeping on the papers on his desk. He talks about life, poetry, cinema, literature, religion, art, and love. What about architecture? "I chose it because it strikes me as a field that brings together all the humanistic disciplines. For me, architecture is emotional. You need to be able to feed yourself on anything else and then reason about space."

Preceding pages: In the courtyard, which is over-looked by the kitchen and the studio of Fabio Novembre, there is a Judas tree that blooms in the spring. On the pillar, or column, which is a symbol of the tree in the Garden of Eden, the initials of Fabio and Candela are engraved in a heart made of white gold mosaic tiles. The entrance has an unusual wrought-iron railing, depicting the primordial serpent as it takes form out of chaos: it is by the artist Duilio Forte, who also decorated the entire wall of the courtyard with iron branches-qua-trellis, which hold up the climbing roses. Among the real roses is a rose made of Murano glass that Fabio Novembre commissioned for the Blumarine stores in Asia.

Left: At the foot of the staircase that leads up to the studio is Fabio Novembre's old BMW motorcycle.
Above: Fabio Novembre, sitting in the box made of plastic reinforced by incorporated fiberglass, *Dream Machine*, by Atelier van Lieshout.
Opposite: Fabio Novembre's studio, which has a floor made of teak, is located in one of the two lofts in the industrial shed. Over the *Smorfia* (Grimace) chair, by Gaetano Pesce, produced by Meritalia, there dominates the protective head of a metal serpent which Novembre made, in collaboration with Tom Dixon. The shape of the worktable, designed by Novembre, is inspired by the isle of Capri: it has a briar-root surface and a base in Bisazza mosaic tile. It is surrounded by *Panton Chairs* by Verner Panton, produced by Vitra. The daisies on the walls are a decorative element that Fabio designed for the Café Atlantique. On the right, is a photograph of Tazio Secchiaroli photographing Fellini, purchased by Novembre with his first earnings.

" In this space I feel free.
I work for myself and with myself.
I need nothing and no one,
but I am not isolated from the world.
I feel isolated from disturbances,
from distortions, from paranoias. "

MICHELE
DE LUCCHI

Michele De Lucchi was born in 1951 in Ferrara and took his degree in architecture in Florence. In the years of Radical Architecture, he was a leading figure in such movements as Cavart, Alchimia, and Memphis. He designed furniture for the best-known Italian and European manufacturers. He developed projects for Compaq, Philips, Siemens, and Vitra and was the director of Olivetti Design from 1992 until 2002, working on a number of personal theories about the evolution of the workplace. He designed and renovated buildings in Japan for NTT, in Germany for the Deutsche Bank, in Switzerland for Novartis, and in Italy for ENEL, Telecom Italia, and Piaggio. Since 1999 he has been working on the repurposing of a number of electric power stations for ENEL Produzione. He worked on the development of the image for Deutsche Bank, Deutsche Bundesbahn, ENEL, Poste Italiane, Telecom Italia, Banca Popolare di Lodi, Banca 121, and Banca Intesa. He has overseen installations of art and design exhibitions and has designed installations for museums such as the Milan Triennale, the Permanente of Milan, the Palazzo delle Esposizioni in Rome, and the Neues Museum in Berlin. In 1990 he founded Produzione Privata, a small company for which Michele De Lucchi designed products made

Michele De Lucchi has a special place that he created to spend time undisturbed and think about his design projects. Il Chioso is in Angera, on Lake Maggiore, not far from where he lives. But unlike his professional studios in Milan and Rome, which are filled with people and problems, "Il Chioso is my personal studio—and it resembles me to a degree—where I think, draw, sculpt, take pictures, paint, and live. At Il Chioso nobody can see me, nobody can hear me. Sometimes I gather my courage and sing," De Lucchi tells us. "In this space I feel free. I work for myself and with myself. I need nothing and no one, but I am not isolated from the world. I feel isolated from disturbances, from distortions, from paranoias." De Lucchi is an architect and industrial designer who has designed objects that are world famous: the *Tolomeo* (Ptolemy) lamp, designed for Artemide in 1987, is still in production and very popular for use in public and private spaces. A protagonist of the experimental architecture of Alchimia and Memphis, he was put in charge of the Olivetti Design department in 1992. He created the new image of the Poste Italiane, or Italian post office, Telecom Italia, and many banks, including Banca Intesa, Deutsche Bank,

and the electric power plants of ENEL. He renovated the former complex of GUM department stores on Red Square. And yet he confesses, "In the end, this is not just the work of an architect or a designer, it is also the work of an artist."

The name Il Chioso comes from the fact that it is enclosed (*chiuso*) by high old stone walls that once protected the area set aside for fruit and vegetable gardens for the inhabitants of Angera. Then it became a huge henhouse and, in 1951—the year De Lucchi was born—it was transformed into a warehouse for a building company that is no longer in business. De Lucchi found it in a state of total neglect and abandonment: a large cement shed; a long, large open portico; a very long, smaller portico; and a small house in a corner. All these buildings, erected along the walls, overlook a central meadow. It is all very snug and close: "It feels as if you are in the cloister of a monastery," says De Lucchi. He did not change the general layout of the buildings, but he restructured them and made a road that links them together. It is here that he developed his love for woodworking, the rediscovery of manual work. "Il Chioso had been the warehouse of a construction company, and I found a great

quantity of wood here for scaffolding, and I needed to do something with it. I began by purchasing a chainsaw… I started making little men, little miniature men, but I wasn't very good at it. I'm not a sculptor. The constant theme of my work, however, is space for humans, and so I began carving houses, little houses that, right from the beginning, turned out much better than the little men."

Perhaps he was inspired by the little house of Il Chioso, which once served as a tool shed and as a shelter against summer thunderstorms. Today it is a small and very romantic residence, where De Lucchi has frequently spent the night. It has only a single bedroom, a bathroom, and a veranda with glass walls, which offers a fine view of all of Il Chioso.

There is a photograph depicting him seated in front of the door of this little fairy-tale house: "I have always been fascinated by the character of the old Chinese man in love, abandoned by his wife, silent and discreet, who appears, sitting in front of his little house in the woods, in the movie *Dersu Uzala* by Kurosawa." But De Lucchi has not been abandoned: he has a German wife and four children, and yet he manages to spend at least

one day a week in this place outside of the world, as well as some time on weekends, during the Christmas and Easter holidays, and in the summer. He says that Il Chioso is a sort of extension of his own home, an appendage to that house; in fact, it is his second home.

When he took over Il Chioso there were already a number of large trees: oak trees, hazels, persimmons, japonicas, and rhododendrons: he planted nine cypress trees in front of his studio. A sheltered sunny corner behind his studio is the camellia garden: all of them are rare plants, collection-worthy, and De Lucchi loves them very much. The soil around the lake is especially acidic and well suited to growing this plant, which produces spectacular blooms in the springtime.

His studio, which is located in the large long shed, has seven huge windows on each side and a zinc roof supported by steel I-beams. On the interior, it is a large, single open space with a raised floor and a long curving walls that serves as a partition and as a bookcase: it is all made with the unfinished wood of construction-yard boards that were left behind when the builder abandoned the place. Adjoining the studio, in a large structure with twelve huge windows and thirteen

with artisanal techniques and workmanship. A selection of his objects has been displayed in the most important museums in Europe, the United States, and Japan. In 2001, he was appointed full professor in the Department of Design and the Arts at the Istituto Universitario di Architettura (University Institute of Architecture) in Venice. In 2006 he received an honorary doctorate from Kingstone University.

Preceding pages, left: Michele De Lucchi hand carves wood beneath the portico of Il Chioso, using traditional tools or a chainsaw. Wood is the material he uses to develop his designs and is a basic element in his architectural work.
Preceding pages, right: Beneath the portico of Il Chioso are piles of logs, used to feed the fireplace in the adjoining cottage.

Above, left: A view of the main complex that was used as a henhouse until the fifties. It was renamed Il Chioso because it is surrounded by high enclosure walls that isolate the complex from the town of Angera. On the left, the shed that is used as a private studio and, adjoining it, the shed that houses De Lucchi's archives; together, they enclose a garden space with three persimmon trees at the center.
Above: The portico that contains the workshop, as seen from the cottage.

pillars made of unfinished iron, is the designer's archive, with all the models of his architectural and design projects; also stored here are his drawings, paintings, posters, and photographs. A very orderly space, with everything lined up neatly on long shelves: "The archive is useful for finding quickly everything or anything that is in it, and I am so terrified by all the confusion that I have in my head, by messiness, by doubts, by uncertainties. I manage to design orderly spaces but I can never manage to bring order to my sensations and feelings."

But the most fascinating part of Il Chioso is unquestionably the smaller portico, which comprises thirty-two columns and which runs all around the enclosure walls, over the place where the hill rises toward the famous old castle, the Rocca di Angera; it now serves as an exhibition space for prestigious shows. It is very long, and it follows the lie of the inclined land: "I use it to take walks, so that I can stroll without getting lost while I am thinking," says the designer. Beneath the portico of Il Chioso, there are stacks of cut logs that are used to feed the fireplace of the adjoining little house, as well as other pieces of wood, ready to be carved. Wood is the material in

which De Lucchi develops his projects. Slowly, by hand, he works the raw wood, sculpting it, and finishing it with enormous patience and skill. He is fascinated by the skill of craftsmen. "Everything begins with the hands: they are the closest thing we have to our brains because the path from the idea to the hand is always the shortest path that exists. Using a computer does not always shorten that distance."

De Lucchi is an entrepreneur who manufactures the lamps, furniture, and glass vases that he has designed for his own company, Produzione Privata (literally, "private production"). Since 2003, Michele De Lucchi has begun an exploration of the idea of conceiving architecture as sculpture. This was the origin of the first series of the *Casette* (literally, "cottages" or "little houses"), sculptures done with a chainsaw and then further refined with traditional tools. The second series, *Geometrie* (Geometries), focuses on the material in its purest essence. The last series has an orotund name: *Muri e Strutture Eroiche* (Walls and Heroic Structures): "In architecture, there is always a heroic aspect that needs to emanate from the walls and structures."

Opposite: A short path leads from the garden to another raised green area, where the cottage is located. In order to reach the cottage, it is necessary to pass between the tall oak trees that separate De Lucchi's working life from his more contemplative life. From the cottage, a small hut with a fireplace, it is possible to take in the view of the entire complex.

Above: Michele De Lucchi sitting on the threshold of the cottage, once a storehouse for tools, and today a small residence. On the pergola in front of the door, in the spring, a beautiful wisteria blooms.

Above, right: In the main building, used as a private studio, there are two small rooms in the rear, which share the same continuous walls of glass looking out onto the enclosure wall. One room is used as a kitchen, the other as a bathroom. On the wall of the bathroom, across from the bathtub, is a large mirror without a frame hanging over the Duravit washbasin. A wooden bench serves as a towel rack, and above the mirror is the *Acquaparete* (Water Wall) lamp, made of Murano glass, designed by De Lucchi for Produzione Privata, 1998. The faucets are by Dornbracht.

Overleaf, left: A detail of *Geometria*. In 2003 Michele De Lucchi began to reflect on the possibility of treating architecture as sculpture. Two years later he presented the *Casette* series, delicately cut sculptures in wood made with an electric saw.

Overleaf, right: The studio also functions as a gallery for sculptures, scale models, and designs of works in progress. In the foreground are pieces from various series of works including *Geometrie*, *Casette*, and *Muri e Strutture Eroiche*. The spaces in Il Chioso are well adapted for creating and displaying the work of De Lucchi. Next to *Muro Eroico n. 4*, in birchwood, is a photograph of Tolstoy. Drawings of projects hang on a long curved wall that also serves to separate the studio from the kitchen and bathroom.

Above, left: The tall dark curtains at the back of the studio separate the design area from the area that can be converted, when necessary, into a set, where Michele De Lucchi photographs his creations for Produzione Privata. In the foreground, a number of *2001* chairs, designed by Michele De Lucchi for Produzione Privata.

Above, right: The natural light from the large windows on the wall is augmented by a series of spotlights and hanging lamps over the worktables. An enfilade of worktables and drawing boards leads all the way to Michele De Lucchi's table, separated from the entrance by a large bookcase/wall made of wood.

Opposite: Through the main door is a space with a cot, a tripod, and the prototype of a wood and metal bench. Near the large window are two armchairs designed by Michele De Lucchi for the interior of the Manager Restaurant NTT in Tokyo in 1991, produced by Cassina Japan. Along the wall is a wooden bracket where De Lucchi leans and hangs *objets trouvés*.

Overleaf left: The bookcase behind Michele De Lucchi's worktable is a haven for objects, tools, and photographs. Here—amid the books, boxes, and photograph albums—are notebooks, large and small, where with India ink, pencils, and watercolors he records his story and the stories of his projects. On the top shelf are two photographs, one of Henri Matisse and the other of the Jewish Museum in Berlin, by Daniel Libeskind. The lamp in the foreground is the *Tolomeo* (Ptolemy), designed by De Lucchi for Artemide in 1987.

Overleaf, right: On top of the bookcase, De Lucchi has set aside a special place for his collection of his Christmas vases, made to his designs by Produzione Privata. These are small glass vases made in different shapes and colors, each year dedicated to a different plant, which is selected and then stylized in the form of a small metal branch, *the olive* in 2001, *the peony* in 2004, *the lemon* in 2005, and so on in the years to come.

" *I fell in love with the view: the park,
the Torre Branca by Gio Ponti,
the tree-lined boulevard, and the mountains.* **"**

BOB
NOORDA
ORNELLA
NOORDA

Bob Noorda was born in Amsterdam and has pursued a career in the fields of visual communication, corporate identity, packaging, product design, and interior decoration. He has received numerous awards and prizes, including four Golden Compass awards: in 1964 for the signage of the Metropolitana subway system of Milan, in 1979 for the symbol and image of the Region of Lombardy, in 1984 for the coordinated image of Fusital, and in 1994 for his career. He was also awarded a gold medal in Rimini for his work in the field of design. In 1961 he was the art director of the Pirelli corporation. From 1979 to 1992 he was the art director of the Touring Club of Italy. He designed the trademarks of Mondadori, Ricordi Mediastore, Total Italia, Touring Club Italiano (Touring Club of Italy), ENEL, Zucchi, Valli & Valli, and Feltrinelli. He was a professor of graphics at the Umanitaria of Milan, the I.S.I.A. (Istituto Superiore per le Industrie Artistiche, or Higher Institute for Artistic Industries) in Urbino and at the I.E.D. (Instituto Europeo di Design, or European Design Institute) in Milan; from 1996 to 2001 he was a professor of visual communications in the department of design at the Politecnico, or Polytechnic University, of Milan. In 2005 he was given an honorary doctorate in Design by the Politecnico of Milan.

Ornella and Bob Noorda are both architects and designers, and are a couple in both life and work. They live in Milan, on the top floor of a nine-teenth-century *palazzo*: the windows of their apartment, a two-story penthouse, overlook the greenery of the Parco Sempione. "This is why I chose this apartment: for the view of the park, which changes color with the seasons and always has a different sort of charm. I fell in love with the view: the park, the Torre Branca by Gio Ponti, the tree-lined boulevard, and the mountains. On the clearest days, I can even make out Mount Rosa." Ornella Noorda is Milanese. She designs lamps, jewelry, carpets, tiles, and decorative objects; she also does interior design, product design, and graphic design. She was very young when she met her husband, Bob, a Dutch designer who came to Italy to work as the art director for Pirelli, in the sixties. Bob Noorda was responsible for all the signage of the Metropolitana subway system in Milan and the subway system in São Paulo, Brazil. He has also designed many famous trademarks and logos, and he has won an impressive four Golden Compass awards for his designs.

They are an elegant and likable couple, and they already have a granddaughter, Viola, who

spends a lot of time here, playing. "We argue about everything, constantly," says Ornella of her husband. "Maybe that's why we've been together for so long."

The apartment, which extends over two stories, demanded an enormous amount of time and money for the renovation. It took long years of work because this space was originally a small apartment with an attic in a state of complete disrepair. At the beginning Ornella, who lived a short walk away, in her family home, had thought of using it for her studio but, she explains: "In the end, we reversed things: we left the studio where we were living and moved our home here." But Ornella had to fight the matter through with Bob, who was opposed to getting trapped in the "endless" renovation work that was necessary. He was very familiar with his wife's perfectionism, and she oversaw every detail with painstaking care. "I demolished all of the interior walls, saving only the old roof beams. Once those had been carefully and thoroughly sanded, they were reinforced with steel I-beams concealed in the walls. And I redesigned the whole space; I really wanted to achieve a sense of vertical space and openness, so I created an open loft with a glass balustrade

to render the space transparent, allowing in plenty of light."

The kitchen is tiny; it's practically a cooking corner, separated from the living room: "We like to eat in the kitchen and we don't need anything big: just the bare necessities so that we can cook something. All the rest, the china, the pots and pans, and the drinking glasses, I put in a large antique armoire in the living room."

Already, from the entry area, with its walls lined with books, which opens out onto the large light-filled living, you notice the exquisite eighteenth-century Chinese panels, so large that a wall was custom-built to hold them. "I didn't want to give them up. They are a family heirloom, and they are very precious. I had always seen them in my home since I was a little girl, and I was attached to them. But moving them was a problem: I had to cut out a section of a beam to fit them in." The placement of these panels painted with scenes of Chinese life determined the composition of the rest of the space, which was shaped to highlight their presence. Even the structure of the loft with the beams painted red was designed to pick out certain points of red in the paintings. Such an imposing presence was not

to be disturbed by other pieces of antique furniture. Therefore, they chose linear items, design classics, such as the café table by Eileen Gray or the Eames armchair or the oval table, a piece of Scandinavian design by Eero Saarinen for Knoll, which alone dominates the center of the room. Special care was devoted to the choice of materials: the "gymnasium" flooring is a parquet made of durmast wood, finished in an unusual manner to provide a bamboo effect. In the bathroom there is a stone from the Apuan Alps, a stone left unfinished, with lovely pink and green veins; Ornella and Bob found it in a quarry and selected the exact veins that they wanted: "This stone is so beautiful; it looks like an endpaper from an antique book binding." The stairs, which lead to the upper story, are also made of a stone from the Apuan Alps, a stone called Cardoso.

The love that the Noordas feel for the East, where they have visited repeatedly on their travels, emerges in the furnishings and in the form of the rooms. The sliding, Japanese-style doors are made of wood and a plastic material that seems like paper. The red-lacquered kimono stand in the bedroom is also Japanese. The small benevolent Buddha head that guards the entrance to the

Ornella Noorda founded Unimark International in 1965 with Bob Noorda. She later opened a consulting studio of her own: Noorda Design. She has designed exhibitions, installations, and shops. She has also created collections in silver and gold. Since 1989 she has held a chair in packaging at the Istituto Europeo di Design. For Edilnord she designed the Sporting Club of Milan 2, where she designed all the furniture. In 1968 she participated in the Fourteenth Milan Triennale with the installation Il posto della immaginazione. *She has participated in many exhibitions in Italy and internationally: at the Museum of the Twentieth Century in Vienna, at the Twenty-Fifth Venice Biennale (in the glassmaking section), at the Museum of Modern Art in New York, at the Galleria Marconi in Milan, at Palazzo Strozzi in Florence, and elsewhere.*

Preceding pages, left: Bob and Ornella Noorda, seen from the loft above them. They are sitting on an Eames *Lounge Chair and Ottoman*. The café table made of glass and steel is by Eileen Gray and the chrome-plated lamp is by Sergio Asti.
Preceding pages, right: The dining area.

Preceding pages, left: The bedroom has a Japanese-style sliding door with a wooden frame and plastic panels that look like paper. At the entrance to the room, an Indian Buddha head. At the foot of the bed, an unusual red-lacquered Japanese kimono valet and a lamp by Muthesius. On the right: The entrance hall, with its walls lined with books, has arched doorways that lead into the living room. The partition, with a mirrored wall, features an artwork by Lucio Fontana and conceals the very small kitchen. Hung as a sculpture, a small inlaid wooden door, typical of the *greniers* of Mali.

Preceding pages, right: The antique eighteenth-century Chinese panels, which belonged to the family of Ornella Noorda, serve as a background to a design classic, the oval table with a marble top by Eero Saarinen for Knoll, 1956. Sitting atop the table is a Burmese container. The transparent chairs are the *La Marie* model, by Philippe Starck for Kartell. The hanging lamp made of blown glass is the simple *Sirio* (Sirius) by Solzi Luce, which hangs from the very high ceiling on a red wire.

Opposite: The staircase that leads up to the loft is made of unfinished stone from the Apuan Alps. A small luminous niche lights the staircase and a wooden horse, a souvenir from a trip to India. The painting above the stairs is by Ornella Noorda. The space beneath the stairs is screened by panels that allow light to shine through. The flooring of the apartment is a "gymnasium" parquet made of durmast, processed for a bamboo effect.

Above: A view of the penthouse living room on the top floor, with antique beams that have been reinforced with steel I-beams.

Above, right: A part of the living area with an eighteenth-century marble bust, an antique family console that contrasts in a pleasant way with Ornella Noorda's red painting.

Overleaf, left: In illuminated niches cut into the shape of the roof, there is a collection of spheres in all sorts of materials and of all sorts of origins. The little armchairs in the foreground are by Le Corbusier, 1928.

Overleaf, right: In one of the windows looking out onto the patio, there is a statue of the "wind god," brought from Mexico. It is decorative and brings good omens. The Iranian red wool carpet, the *Gabbeh* by Yaky, Milan, is a gift from Bob to Ornella.

nighttime living area is Indian, while the antique door carved in relief comes from Mali; it was purchased in adventuresome circumstances and hung on the wall as a sculpture: "These little doors in Mali are typical of the greniers, you can hardly find them anymore because they have been bought up so extensively by antiques dealers." Ornella tells amusing anecdotes about the hunt for and purchase of each object.

Ornella wanted to bring as much light as possible into the penthouse, and she managed to do it with clever design and construction techniques. Now she calls this apartment "the house of light." On the top story, light spreads everywhere, thanks to a glass door that opens out onto an astonishing "Mediterranean" terrace with lemon trees, rosebushes, and bunches of rosemary and other aromatic herbs. This is a relaxing corner where it is possible to enjoy a cup of tea on a café table from a Greek tavern or else relax on a large sofa made of black cast iron, originally from India. But it is the small courtyard, transformed into a patio, luxuriant with rare succulents from Asia and Peru, that brings light to the entire living room. "I brought this elephant-ear palm all the way from Hawaii. I carried it in my arms," explains

Ornella who, carried away by her enthusiasm, brought back from Mexico a statue of a wind god; it was packed amateurishly and it arrived in pieces. Bob restored it with painstaking care, and now the statue dominates a window facing out onto the patio.

The loft has a quality of lightness and is practically transparent: the railing on the staircase is made of glass, as is the table designed by Asnago and Vender, while the transparent chairs are by Philippe Starck for Kartell. The light is multiplied by mirrors of various sizes that illuminate every corner. In the penthouse, the apartment becomes an intimate space. Books, photographs of their children, antique heirloom furniture, informal paintings by Ornella, *objets trouvés* such as the vast collection of spheres in all hues and materials, glass, marble, papier-mâché, and semi-precious stones.

Bob is leaving for Canada, and Ornella will have to wait for him to get back before leaving on a trip to Cuba: their cat cannot be left alone. The Noordas are curious, careful travelers: and here, as if in a treasure chamber, they gather the fruit of their tireless quests.

" *The way you dress corresponds reasonably closely to the way you live: you present yourself as you are. It is like a calling card. Your clothing, like your home, says a great deal about you. It reveals a lot about who you are.* "

VICO
MAGISTRETTI

Vico Magistretti was born in Milan in 1920. He took a degree in architecture in 1945 after having studied at the Champ Universitaire Italien in Lausanne. He is one of the founding fathers of Italian design, and since 1948 he has participated in the various of the Milan Triennale. In 1956 he was one of the founders of ADI (Associazione per il Disegno Industriale, or Association for Industrial Design). He has designed objects, lamps, and pieces of furniture for Cassina, Artemide, Fritz Hansen, De Padova, Kartell, FontanaArte, Flou, Oluce, Campeggi, and Poltrona Frau. He has taught at the Royal College of Art in London. His design products are featured in the permanent collections of the most important museums in the world, including twelve objects in the collection of the Museum of Modern Art in New York. He has received numerous recognitions and awards for his work, including the Golden Compass in 1967 for the Eclisse (Eclipse) lamp and the Golden Compass for his career, in 1995. In 2003 he was the subject of a major exhibition at the Palazzo Ducale in Genoa. Alongside his work as an industrial designer, he has had a career as an architect. He is currently developing plans for a residential village for Schiffini in Ceparana, La Spezia, and the expansion and renovation of the former Cerruti mills in Biella.

One feels a sense of excitement and joy when entering the home of Vico Magistretti, particularly at the sight of the spectacular patio filled with green plants and white flowers, the favorite flowers of the master of the house. The patio is the true fulcrum of the apartment. Magistretti designed this space by cutting into the roof to create a central point of light. The entire living area radiates around the patio, which illuminates every corner. Family is important to Magistretti, who keeps photographs of his parents on the *Nuvola Rossa* (Red Cloud) bookcase that he designed for Cassina. His father was a very well known architect working in Milan during the first half of the twentieth century. He was named Piergiulio Magistretti, and he designed many of the *palazzi* in the center of the city. The piece of American office furniture—next to the table where Vico Magistretti works—belonged to his father. "I like this piece of furniture so much that I wish I had designed it. I find it appropriate that in a home there should also be pieces of the past, the history of a person. But I only need a few things to remember."

This home is very Milanese—very much like him, "il Vico," as his Milanese-style nickname goes; Vico Magistretti is a seventh-generation Milan native, one of the few who can still speak perfect Milanese dialect, with a faint air of Milanese snobbishness.

He has lived in this penthouse apartment for more than twenty years. He is an architect and was one of the founding fathers of Italian design in the years following World War II. Vico Magistretti is by now a living legend. He is responsible for innovations that have changed the way many people live. One need only think of his little lamp, the *Eclisse* (Eclipse) by Artemide; in the sixties nearly everyone had one. And the *Atollo* (Atoll) lamp by Oluce became a status symbol. Then there is the revolutionary textile bed, the *Nathalie* by Flou, the first bed you could dress and undress as you pleased. "The *Eclisse* represented for me what the *Arco* lamp meant for my very dear friend, Achille Castiglioni, a success that finally turned into something close to a nuisance."

This well-proportioned apartment, with its nicely articulated spaces, resembles Magistretti. It has a discreet and refined elegance, it is cultivated but never boring, it has no extraneous decorations but it does have all the key elements of

his personal history: his books, his eighteenth-century paintings, and his works of contemporary art, his beloved Khmer sculptures, music by Bach and Mozart, and of course, many, many design objects that constitute his diary and that tell the story of his lengthy career as a designer. He speaks brusquely about them: "They're here because the companies that manufactured them gave them to me as gifts. In any case, I would never have designed objects that I wouldn't want to have in my own house." In this space, the books are the stars. There are many books, placed just about everywhere, because he has always been a voracious reader. "A house without books already says a great deal about the people who live there." In view on the bookshelf is Tolstoy's *War and Peace*, which he has read at least three times. He used the name of one of the characters, Natasha, or Nathalie, as she is also referred to, at least in the Italian edition, for the famous textile bed he designed for Flou. "In the last chapter of the book, the description of the house of Pyotr, or Pierre, and Natasha, or Nathalie, newlyweds, is a treatise on interior decorating."

Magistretti admits that he has had the good fortune to do the work that he loves: designing objects for mass production. And maybe that is why he just cannot seem to stop inventing new forms and planning things and making sketches everywhere he happens to be. Even now, in a difficult period for him because of problems with his health, he is unfailingly active and inquisitive, he works enthusiastically—together with his assistant, Paolo—on new designs. Work has filled his life and even now it remains an important stimulus. He has just finished designing a glass café table, the *Gemini* for FIAM Italia—which stands on display in the living room—and a "revolutionary" little sofa for Campeggi. He is designing an entire small town for the industrialist Schiffini, near La Spezia, and he proudly shows off the renderings, a little citadel filled with towers and greenery. "I'm working furiously, even though I dream of playing a little golf."

The things he loves most about his home are the continuously changing light, the silence, and the view. "The first time that I climbed up here to look around, I was getting ready to renovate the entire building. I looked out of the windows and I was transfixed: outside you could see the Duomo, or Milan cathedral, and the Madonnina, the statue of the Virgin Mary atop the Duomo.

Preceding pages, left: Vico Magistretti, sitting on a *Carimate* chair, one of his first pieces of design (Cassina, 1959), observes his most recent project, visible in the foreground: the FIAM Italia Gemini café table, 2006, made of two identical superimposed slabs of curved glass.

Preceding pages, right: The patio, seen from the entrance, is the fulcrum of the apartment.

Above: The study area where Magistretti works when he is at home. On the table is the *Atollo* (Atoll) lamp, an icon of Italian design, which he designed for Oluce in 1977. The sofa upholstered in red fabric is the *Sindbad*, for Cassina, 1981. Next to the *Gemini* café table is a *Carimate* chair by Cassina. On the walls, family paintings from the eighteenth century and contemporary informal artworks. Next to the window, a Khmer sculpture and an architectural maquette, a gift from Renzo Piano.

Opposite: The living room as seen from the dining area. Just visible above the sliding glass door is an oculus that allows light to pour in. The patio is a spectacular corner of greenery. At the far end of the room is another terrace that offers a magnificent view down onto the old interior garden.

Preceding pages: Two views of the dining area. The table is one of Magistretti's very first projects, and it is illuminated by the large cupola of the *Sonora* (Sonic) lamp, designed for Oluce in 1974. Around the table are black *Carimate* chairs. A thick slab of black glass serves as a shelf (visible in the image on the left) where Magistretti has placed antique sculptures and small paintings. The collage depicting a woman's face is a gift from the Louisiana Museum in Copenhagen.

Opposite: On a nineteenth-century table that belonged to Vico's father—architect Piergiulio Magistretti—there are books, photographs, and notebooks. The hanging lamp is the *Snow* by Magistretti for Oluce. On the shelf running above the window that looks onto the patio are portraits of Vico Magistretti's great-grandparents and two vases that his father brought back from Paris.
Above: Behind the table is the steel and birchwood chair *Vicosolo*, which forms part of a series of chairs designed by Magistretti for Fritz Hansen. The *Nuvola Rossa* (Red Cloud) bookcase, designed by Magistretti in 1977 for Cassina, serves as a partition between the entrance hall and the living room.
Above, right: The *Nuvola Rossa*. Magistretti is a voracious reader and believes that a home without books is a home without a soul.

You could see the round dome of the church of San Carlo and the gardens of the interior courtyards, so typical of the buildings of the historic center. Outside was my Milan." He admits that this view never ceases to amaze him. Even at the dinner table, he chooses to sit in a strategic position in order to enjoy the view. Above the round dining table, surrounded by his *Carimate* chairs for Cassina, is a large dome lamp, the *Sonora* (Sonic) that he designed for Oluce.

He was curious as a young man, and he still is. He liked to experiment. He was friends with the group of architects who created the history of Italian design in the postwar years, such as Caccia Dominioni, Ignazio Gardella, Marco Zanuso, Achille Castiglioni and his brothers; they were comrades in many adventures. "We were all friends. We practiced the same profession without rivalry because we were creating such different things. We had so much fun together." For years, Vico Magistretti designed furniture and objects for De Padova; he made important contributions to the rejuvenation of the image of this Milanese manufacturer. Maddalena De Padova is his partner in life as well. But she does not live here. This remains a single man's apartment. He

is cared for by his faithful housekeeper, Nelly, who spoils him, baking exquisite cakes for teatime. Magistretti never skips the ritual of teatime: he lived in England for many years, when he was teaching at the Royal College of Art in London, and he has adopted a number of very British habits.

When asked if there is anything in his home that he couldn't live without, he gives a surprising answer: "My custom-built wardrobes for my shirts," and then he bursts into his pleasant laugh. Magistretti has a genuine obsession with bespoke shirts, made in London by Turnbull & Asser, the company that made shirts for Churchill. He has more than a hundred tailor-made shirts, in all colors, in stripes and checks, meticulously arranged on the shelves of his wardrobe, the assortment of a genuine dandy. Another habit of his: he wears red socks. "The way you dress corresponds reasonably closely to the way you live: you present yourself as you are. It is like a calling card. Your clothing, like your home, says a great deal about you. It reveals a lot about who you are."

" *This is the home of my feeling, my thinking,
my living, more than my actual house.
If I have to think of a home,
I think of this studio of mine.* "

RICCARDO
DALISI

*Riccardo Dalisi, born in Potenza in 1931, lives in
Naples, where he teaches industrial design and
architectural planning at the Department of
Architecture of the University of Naples. He is an
eclectic artist and designer, and an unusual figure in
the field of design, where he is known as "the poet"
for his objects and furniture, which evoke the magic
of childhood and dreaming. He has organized
educational events in the poorer quarters of Naples,
staging performances and making use of simple
recycled materials. He founded, in 1973, with
Sottsass, Mendini, and Branzi, a counterschool that
was in the vanguard of architecture and design,
called Global Tools. In those same years, he devoted
himself to the study of Gaudí, the Catalonian master
he admired. In 1979, after being hired by Alessi to
conduct a research project on the Neapolitan
caffettiera, or coffeemaker, he designed one that
would be awarded the Golden Compass in 1981,
along with a number of other prototypes on the
same theme. As an industrial designer, he has
worked with Zanotta, Alessi, Oluce, Fiat, Morphos,
Rex, Slamp, Glas, Bisazza, Eschenbach, Rosenthal,
and others. As a sculptor, he has held major shows
at the Palazzo Reale in Naples and elsewhere.*

Riccardo Dalisi claims that his real home is his studio, where he spends hours and hours every day
and every night, sometimes even on Sundays.
There, he is painting, sculpting, thinking: in other
words, creating those poetic, and oneiric, objects
that form part of his designs. And even resting.
"This is the home of my feeling, my thinking, my
living, more than my actual house. It is a place for
meetings, my wife comes here, some of my children come here. I've even slept here once or
twice. If I have to think of a home, I think of this
studio of mine." There are lots of buried design
objects. Buried as well are works of sculpture,
works of *arte povera*, jewelry from an exhibition,
and masks that were featured in another exhibition at the Teatro Mercadante in Naples.
"Everyone tells me that I am a poet, and that's
fine with me. But in Naples they tell me that I'm
'the guy who made that coffeepot!'" In order to
understand his poetics, it is necessary to enter this
grotto where he takes refuge, where he seeks
peace. Far from the university where he teaches
industrial design in Naples, the city where he has
always lived, far from the world of Milanese
design, alone in his universe of imagination. The
figure of an industrial designer who is inventive

rather than rational, Dalisi is perhaps closer to the
world of art than that of industrial design: a
painter and sculptor of some renown but also,
and especially, a designer whose expressive exploration makes use of symbols inspired by myths
and the world of the sacred, from recycled materials like iron, copper, brass, treated with crafts-
manlike loving care. Perhaps his most famous
design was an odd little coffeemaker that was
produced by Alessi, in 1987, and which formed
part of a collection of more than two hundred
prototype models on the theme. Dalisi won the
Golden Compass award from the ADI, in 1981, for
this research project. "The Neapolitan caffettiera
became a personality, a character. I can't say
whether it was an object of art or an object of
design; I know only that it is a collection of cylin-
ders that made it an animated object." Another
successful product was the *Metopa* (Metope) bed
for Zanotta, which reflects the tradition of
Neapolitan wrought iron and has memorable little figures flying a heart on a string amid the
scrollwork of the headboard.

But all of his designs, whether ironic, playful,
or human, launch messages about the joy of life,
of hopes and dreams. It is no accident that the

designer that Dalisi has studied most thoroughly is the Catalonian architect Gaudí, to whom he feels closest, about whom he wrote a book—Gaudí mobili e oggetti. "As a young man I used to wonder why there had never been a Neapolitan Gaudí," Dalisi says ironically, since he feels that to some degree he is Gaudí's spiritual heir.

To step through the doors of Riccardo Dalisi's Neapolitan studio is to step into a different dimension. The space appears to be chaotic: the work table is completely overwhelmed by piles of papers in which only he could hope to find anything. He sits down, smiling, at his desk, clearing himself a space. "I have a filing system based on disorderliness. I have made dossiers of the various typologies of messiness, which is a special kind of order and organization: things from various periods, made of various materials. Not only can I find everything but sometimes, I intentionally put things just this way. Every so often something will emerge and I remember something I wrote—a letter, things from the past—and I put them together, by chance. Up above, on a loft, are objects made of papier-mâché from the sixties and seventies, a different kind of disorder." Set against the window is a painting that he did on

canvas "which also serves to ward off drafts," says Dalisi, who has done many paintings on canvas and on wrapping paper. From the ceiling, little silhouettes hang, cut out of paper or tin, turning gently in the breeze. Everywhere, in every corner imaginable, there are sculptures, prototypes, paintings, masks, strange figurines, the fruit of his tireless imagination. It is possible to understand many aspects of his design, by observing the collection of objects in his studio: for instance, one can see just how important a factor in his creativity are old materials, manual dexterity, craftsmanship, and the freedom of expression that is found in objects of everyday use. And the degree to which his objects resemble children's games. "I drew closer to my approach to design through my relationship with children. Children have taught me a great deal. I think that children help us to have a sense of humanity and spontaneity. When I became a university professor, I would take my students into the poorer quarters of the city, asking them to bring along their architectural models. Then they would ask children from the neighborhood to draw the models, to reinterpret them. What comes out of this is another perspective, an original point of view—the same project

Preceding pages, left: The architect Riccardo Dalisi and a view of his studio in Naples.
Preceding pages, right: The studio overflows with an apparently random messiness. Hanging from the ceiling and twisting in the breeze are figurines cut out of tin and paper or made of wire, copper, brass, and the unassuming materials that Dalisi prefers. Professor Dalisi's desk is totally submerged by piles of paper.
Above, left: A sculpture by Riccardo Dalisi, made of wrought iron depicting a mother and child; the mother is carrying a bundle of firewood on her head.
Above, right: *Cavallo fiorito* (Flowering Horse), a sculpture/gong cut out from a sheet metal that makes a beautiful sound when struck. Below is an aluminum butterfly-shaped bench, *Mariposa* (Spanish for Butterfly), produced by Zanotta, 1989.
Opposite: In the hallway, one can see the scrollwork headboard of the *Metopa* (Metope) bed, designed by Dalisi for Zanotta, 1989. The papier-mâché lion was made for the traditional Festa dei Gigli (Lily Festival) in Nola during the seventies.

Opposite: The room that houses the workshop where the students from Dalisi's classes do their work.
Above: Even the hallway is filled with a vast array of objects. On the brackets are prototype sculptures, figurines, and masks.

Overleaf, left: A wrought-iron panel, worked in relief, depicting the Crucifixion; it forms part of an entire *Via Crucis* (Stations of the Cross) done for the old Cloister of Santa Chiara, in Naples.
Overleaf, right: "Totocchio"—the name combines the Neapolitan comedian Totò with Pinocchio—is a character about whom Riccardo Dalisi has written storybooks of adventures. Notice the colorful sculpture that forms part of Dalisi's latest research project, *Compassione* (Compassion); it depicts an embrace. The stretched-out hands and the faces are cut out of tin and then colored.

seen with the more spontaneous eyes of a child. I wanted to build a rapport with the people and the city by doing design research and communicating a message. The idea of doing design started in the city, and many of the ideas from there later became industrial design projects." As an industrial designer, Dalisi has worked with some of the best-known companies in the furnishing and furniture: Alessi, Zanotta, Oluce, Slamp, Rex, Bisazza, Baleri, and many others. Wandering through the rooms, one moves past collages, fragments, assemblages of all sorts: a creativity nourished by popular myths and a component of play. The disorder is fascinating, but so is the emotion and the sense of surprise. "The word *Internet* entered my life late: it is a very distant world for me because it is different from the way I think and from my culture, both of which are profoundly linked to the Neapolitan way of being. By climate, character, and tradition I tend to be spontaneous, to communicate with immediacy an idea, perhaps with a sketch, a drawing, a sign, or a form that does not require any explanation. I am certain that technological progress is very useful, but I doubt that it can replace the immediacy of an emotion."

Dalisi is a world-renowned designer, but he describes himself as "a designer of the south" because he continues to work in Naples and has never been willing to leave the city—even though everyone told him that it was impossible to be a designer and live in the south and that it was necessary to move to Milan. "It would have been easier to work in Milan because there are lots of contacts and the design magazines are all published there. But I felt the importance of roots, the strong link with my land and its heritage. I preferred to experiment with recycled materials, the forms of *povero*, or simple, craftsmanship that have survived in the old quarters of the center of Naples." Now he is preparing an exhibition at the Milan Triennale with sculptures sharing the theme of "design and compassion," a research project that he is carrying out in the notorious Rione Sanità, one of the poorest neighborhoods in Naples, where the famous comedian Totò was born, a quarter made famous by Eduardo De Filippo in one of his plays. "*Compassion* in Italian means *con+passione*, that is, 'with+passion,' as well as to share passion, and therefore to share the enormous problems of the Sanità neighborhood, to share this human condition."

MARTINO GAMPER

Martino Gamper was born in Merano in 1971. He studied sculpture at the Academy of Fine Arts of Vienna, product design at the University of Applied Arts in Vienna and at the Royal College of Art in London. He designed tables, chairs, stoves, lamps, cups, children's furniture, bathroom furniture, and benches for public parks. His research resulted in a great many designs for objects that make use of the corners in rooms. He worked in Milan in the studio of Matteo Thun, and in London he has worked with Ron Arad, Tom Dixon, Paul Smith, Michael Craig, Sexymachinery, Jan Family, Kitsune, Retrouvius, and åbäke. He has designed furniture and objects for Thonet, Valli & Valli, Lavazza, Rosenthal, Sexymachinery, British Council, Aram Design, and David Gill. Currently he teaches at the Royal College of Art, in London. He has also taught at the ECAL in Lausanne and at the Ecole des Arts Décoratifs in Paris. Gamper has exhibited his projects at Sotheby's in London, the Oxo Tower in London, the Tallin Art Hall, Bloomberg in London, the Design Museum in London, the Victoria & Albert Museum, the British Council in Milan, the MAK in Vienna, the Kulturhuset Stockholm, the RCA in London, the Memphis-Post Design Gallery in Milan, and the National Museum in Oslo.

Just as non-Italian designers come to Milan and create projects for Italian companies, Italians also leave to seek experience in other countries. Martino Gamper, an Italian designer of the latest generation, has chosen to live in London. "I have found my own space, and it seemed like the right place to carry out my experiments. For the past three years, I have been teaching design at the Royal College of Art. London is a source of inspiration: right now, it is an absolutely stimulating city in terms of creativity and design." Gamper's name appeared in a list of eight stars of new design published by the *Wall Street Journal* in 2005. He is the only Italian who belongs to the new wave of designers who focus on respecting the environment, with a special attention to ecological materials and the importance of recycling. Very relevant topics these days. "I have always loved wood, when I was young I worked as a carpenter in Merano; when I was nineteen, I left and traveled around the world for two years, visiting America, Asia, and Australia, to see what was going on. I was interested in design and art."

Gamper studied sculpture and design in Vienna and had the good fortune to study under artists and designers such as Michelangelo Pistoletto and Ron Arad. In Vienna, he got to know Matteo Thun, who was teaching product design for ceramics and glass at the academy, a decisive encounter. In 1995 he went back to Milan with Thun to work in his studio, where he developed products and objects for WMF, Villeroy & Boch, and Lavazza. It was a great experience, but Gamper immediately understood that if he wanted to grow, he needed to leave. And so he moved to London to study at the Royal College of Art. "Those were two very important years; I got back into touch with Ron Arad and it was then that I developed this passion for corners. It all began with a research project. I was looking for a place to live but couldn't find one. For the time being, I was living in a friend's house, in a corner the size of a broom closet, and I suddenly had the idea that even a tiny hole can become yours if you make good use of a corner. In contemporary design, corners don't get much attention. In London I did my thesis on corners: in any room, there are eight corners that can be exploited. I wrote a whole book about corners. My theory is that a corner should be exploited to the greatest possible degree, especially nowadays, when houses are small and there is not much space."

For his research project on light, Gamper designed a series of neon lamps, which were conceptual pieces. Since space is defined by walls, he created a series of "corner lights" where light defines the space by eliminating empty space.

After taking his degree, he opened a studio and devoted himself to pursuing his "functional" projects, designing a whole series of experimental objects of self-production. "I started to make a few things: an ergonomic tube-sofa that was hollow, a café table that becomes a minibar; I designed a partition screen that is a bookcase on one side and an alcove on the other, then a little sofa that children can use as a toy and even go inside of."

Martino Gamper lives in an industrial space, an open loft, because he loves space. He has furnished it in an alternative style, with the prototypes of his furniture designs. It is the home of a single man, filled with his prototypes, but it is also a cheerful and sociable house: because his love in life is food "and a nice glass of wine," he built a large table, four meters (thirteen feet) long, so that all his friends can come over and share evenings of fine dining. Martino belongs to a generation that places great importance in every-

day living and "design for all," a type of design that is careful to satisfy all requirements. "Design should be more fully integrated with our lives. We are losing touch with the things that we do on a daily basis. Nowadays, everything is done for image, not for our actual everyday life," he explains. "For me, the important things are places, spaces, people, and situations."

He has a notepad full of sketches; he constantly produces new ideas. "I produced the ideas and so many things have emerged as a result." He designed a *Communication Chair*, which is a form of design provocation, but it is also highly functional "performance." Gamper says that "companies are looking for performances." He also decided to design *100 Chairs in 100 Days*, gathering chairs from friends' houses, from the street, from junk shops, and redesigning a new look: a collection of chairs that asks questions about the function of the chair, its use, its purpose.

Gamper is very interested in *materiali poveri*, or simple materials, that he ennobles with other more precious materials. He upholstered an ordinary plastic garden chair in fabric to make it comfortable and elegant. "Design needs to be more honest. We are always trying to hide things;

Preceding pages, left: Martino Gamper gardens in his green "oasis," in the courtyard of his home, in the Hackney Central neighborhood, in London. He found the orange chairs in a junk shop, while the teardrop shaped table is a self-produced prototype. Parked in a corner of his courtyard is his Moulton Mini bicycle.
Preceding pages, right: The building is clearly of industrial origin; it has a brick façade and the distinctive paned windows of a factory.

Above: The interior is formed by a large open space with an open kitchen. Adjoining it are the bedrooms and the utility rooms. The protagonist of the space is the table, four meters (thirteen feet) long, made of repurposed teak, which Gamper found at Retrouvious in London. A few of the chairs surrounding the table are from the *100 Chairs in 100 Days* collection. The two soccer-ball lamps, *Coming Home*, are by Martino Gamper and Rainer Spehl, 2006.
Opposite: Greenery and nature are integral parts of Gamper's design philosophy, as is good food and wine.

Preceding pages, left: A painting inspired by the corner furniture of Gamper, *Corners and More*, was done by åbäke in 2001.

Preceding pages, right: The simple and linear kitchen opens out into the living area. Gamper believes that cooking is a ritual to be shared with his guests in order to spend time together.

Opposite: The bedroom. The red plastic *Arnold Circus Stool* is a design by Martino Gamper. Above the bed is the *Light Together* lamp, also by Gamper.

Below: A hallway that leads to a room filled with chairs and prototypes.

Right: On the mirrored ceiling of the bedroom is an installation, *Cuts*, in acrylic, by Tatiana Grinberg.

Overleaf, left: Chairs from the collection *100 Chairs in 100 Days*, a self-production by Gamper, 2005–06.

Overleaf, right: Top: A bowl found in Morocco; the blown-glass carafe, *Acqua Minerale* (Mineral Water), a self-production; the soccer-ball lamp. Center: Different chairs from the collection *100 Chairs in 100 Days*; candle-holder, *Screwing in Steel*, another self-production; tubular sofa, *The Log*, a tree branch upholstered in leather, by Martino Gamper and Rainer Spehl; wall covering with *Salamandra Forata Bianca* (Perforated White Salamander). Bottom: a prototype of a chair; a small table in the shape of a fox, called *Fox*, covered with printed adhesive by Martino Gamper, Rainer Spehl, and åbäke; a corner of the kitchen where one finds, among other objects, a classic Neapolitan *caffettiera*.

instead, there is so much to be expressed. It is all part of the reuse of design objects created by others."

There are things that go well beyond issues of function, such as *Woodlands*, an installation of stools at the headquarters of Bloomberg in London; *Waste to Taste*, presented at an exhibition of contemporary design at Sotheby's in London; or the *Sit Together Bench*, which won the Oxo Peugeot Design Award in 2003 in the furniture category.

The British Council asked him to do a show, and to design a movable bookcase for traveling. This resulted in the *Book Corner*, with velvet-covered shelves so that it is less likely to get scratched in transit; another advantage is that the books won't slip and slide. This project was presented at the Salone del Mobile, or furniture fair, in Milan.

Especially interesting is the potential of the "recycled" design of remakes. Gamper explored this idea with his close friend Rainer Spehl in the project *We Make Remake* in 2002. They exhibited and sold more than fifty one-off pieces of furniture at the Petrified show, in London.

After making informative visits to the Salone del Mobile in Milan, the Tokyo Design Week, the International Contemporary Furniture Fair in New York, and to 100% Design in London, Gamper believes strongly that the future of design will need to take into account a new generation of objects. He is increasingly convinced that it is important to produce for everyday life, and not for image. "I am interested in the social vision of design: for me, the industrial context is not important. My main reason for making furniture is so that people can use it. Objects have to do with us, with our lives: the formal appearance, the method of production, the relationship with industry, the commercial aspect are an entirely different matter."

" *Water has always been a protagonist
of this building, and because of its size,
it always made me think of a
cathedral of water.* "

STEFANO
GIOVANNONI
ELISA
GIOVANNONI

Stefano Giovannoni, born in La Spezia in 1954, took his degree at the Department of Architecture in Florence in 1978. From 1979 to 1991 he taught and did research at the Department of Architecture in Florence; he was a professor in the master's course at Domus Academy, and at the Università del Progetto in Reggio Emilia; he also served as professor of industrial design at the Università di Architettura, or university department of architecture, in Genoa. He works as an industrial designer, interior decorator, and architect, and he specializes in plastic products. He has collaborated with companies such as Alessi, Cedderoth, Deborah, Flos, Hannstar, Helit, Inda, Kankio, Laufen, Lavazza, Magis, Nissan, Oras, Oregon Scientific, Seiko, Siemens, 3M, and others. He is married to Elisa Giovannoni, who is also his professional partner. She was born in Pordenone, and after specializing at the Scuola Politecnica di Design, she worked with Michele De Lucchi from 1985 to 1989. She works as a designer in the Giovannoni Design Studio in Milan and teaches courses in design at the Scuola Politecnica and at Domus Academy. She works with such corporations as Alessi, Metals, Bisazza, Viceversa, and Ycami.

The house in Milan where Elisa and Stefano Giovannoni live is an example of a home/work-shop, a house-qua-location: an unusual space where everyday life merges with social life. A very modern way of living, without clear bound-aries. The house has become what it currently is after an extraordinary drama, a lengthy restora-tion, with obstacles and detours of every sort, all of which demanded a fair amount of intuition, courage, patience, and faith—gifts that the own-ers of the house possess in considerable measure.

Elisa Giovannoni tells the story of how she suggested to her husband, Stefano, that they repaint their house and also do a little renovation work. He replied that the time had come to move, to look for another, bigger house that was better suited to their lifestyle. They began a painstaking search to find the right space and happened upon a former industrial building, a factory building where the enormous Riva water turbines for ships were tested. The entire interior space was filled with hydraulic machinery, concrete architectural elements, cast-iron structures, giant pipes and tubes, basins, staircases, and ladders. Surely, a building of that sort would suggest anything other than a home. Many people had seen the

building and decided not to take on the chal-lenge. The renovation was rife with obstacles and pitfalls—practical, technical, and bureaucratic. Not to mention the time and costs involved.

The most serious problem was the demoli-tion. The Giovannonis are both people who love a challenge. They didn't let doubts overwhelm them, and they quickly decided to go ahead and buy the building. "It came out of the blue for both of us: we were both immediately attracted to this unusual space. In the early days we looked around in some confusion: the floor below the ground floor was completely filled with water so we couldn't see what was in there. The corner tower contained an enormous water tank. But we were attracted by the forties-style architecture, the red brick, and the high windows made of reinforced concrete and glass tiles," Elisa and Stefano remember. After having checked with engineers and experts in the city government to obtain the various permits that were required, they set to work. They decided to organize the space on three stories: on the ground floor, with its ten-meter ceilings, they decided to create an open space and had the brilliant idea of convert-ing it into a "location" for social and cultural

Preceding pages, left: Stefano and Elisa Giovannoni photographed in the living room of their Milanese home, next to a sixteenth-century picture frame that contains the graphic manipulation of a painting by Giorgione on PVC.
Preceding pages, on the right: The elevator is painted in fluorescent hues.

Opposite: An unusual table made of molave wood from the Philippines, under the *Pillow Talk* glass-and-steel hanging lamp by Johanna Grawunder for Design Gallery, Milano. The two *Big Shadow* standing lamps are by Marcel Wanders.
Above: The living room looks out onto an interior patio, around which the entire home radiates. The furnishings consist of the *On the Rocks* sofas by Francesco Binfaré for Edra and café tables by Ettore Sottsass for the *Bharata* collection of Design Gallery, Milano. Beneath the sixteenth-century picture frame are two *Mademoiselle* chairs, designed by Philippe Starck for Kartell.

Overleaf: The living room enjoys a view onto the greenery of the patio; the artwork at the far end of the room is a painting by Daniele Innamorato. In the foreground is a glass plate by Emanuel Babled.

events. The second floor was made into a professional studio, with a privileged view of the space beneath. And the third story, which once contained the offices of the engineers who were in charge of monitoring the turbines, became their living space. So what should they do with the basement? Considering the number of tanks and basins to catch the water, which came roaring and splashing down from above whenever the turbines were being tested, they decided to convert the basement into a small "spa," with a swimming pool, a sauna, and a laundry room.

"Water has always been a protagonist of this building, and because of its size, it always made me think of a cathedral of water," explains Stefano Giovannoni, who was born in La Spezia. "I was born at the beach, and water is an element that has always been especially fascinating to me. And here I could finally have a kitchen all to myself, because I love to cook fish and I buy very large fish. I designed a 'seafood kitchen,' with an especially deep sink, more than a meter in length where I have fun preparing the fish and then, with all the right equipment, cooking it." This second kitchen is located in the corner tower (twenty-seven meters, or nearly ninety feet, tall)

and it looks out onto the rooftop terrace, where Stefano can serve his dishes to his guests in the dining area beneath the pergola.

The idea of the terrace came as a way of taking advantage of the flat roof, with an area of four hundred square meters (4,300 square feet). Elisa subdivided it into various zones: a corner for sunbathing beneath a trellis, a corner for relaxing, a dining area, and a living room. "The only thing that I regret is the teak covering, which is extremely durable and serves to insulate from the heat, but unfortunately is ill suited to a city like Milan. I hadn't expected it to get so dirty." At the center of the terrace, a patio has been created to bring light down into the residence below, creating a little green spot, around which the apartment radiates. "Thanks to the many outside windows, the house had perhaps even too much light, but what it lacked was an open point of greenery and nature, where it was possible to watch the seasons change. This internal 'garden,' alters the point of view of the house, one can enjoy a view of a wall of jasmine, a pomegranate tree, and an olive tree from every room." The home is practically one open space. The largest area contains the living room and the kitchen;

the bedrooms are distributed around the perimeter. "We liked this quality of circularity: we made all the paths and circulation start from the patio. We wanted to create a neutral shell into which we could insert furniture and objects, to play with color and to create other smaller environments, such as the library and the bathrooms, each of which has a different color," explains Stefano Giovannoni, who is very keen to invoke the memory of his teacher and mentor, Remo Buti, who, during his university years in Florence, imparted to him a design rigor and a minimalism that he has always kept in mind, even in his most playful design work. Giovannoni designed some of the icons of Alessi's production, such as the series—designed with Guido Venturini—called *Girotondo* (named after an Italian children's song and game, roughly equivalent to *Ring Around the Rosie*), featuring a little man cut out in a simple form in steel. Or the objects made of plastic, ironic and transgressive: the *Coccodandy* (Cock-a-Dandy) eggholder, the *Merdolino* bath brush, or the *Pino* funnel.

"I am interested in design as a factor in mass consumption: designing objects for everyone has always been one of my goals. The fact that these are commercial objects means that these products have succeeded in communicating something. They are valid inasmuch as they sell something, for their qualities of appeal and emotion. Behind that is technology, marketing, and everything else. But what counts most is that these are neither status symbols nor style symbols; it is only merchandise that communicates in a direct way."

The Giovannonis named their building the Officine Stendhal, after the name of the street on which it is located, Via Stendhal: "In order to emphasize that the place where we live and work reflects the idea of a workshop, an *officina*, or atelier, of ideas and creativity. In the end, what we do here is to create a series of prototypes."

They never would have imagined that the neighborhood where their *officina* is located would within a few years become the center for so many events, a trendy area where Armani and Della Valle stage runway presentations. "The house became a way of socializing, establishing new contacts, and meeting interesting people, as well as an opportunity for continuous self-regeneration. Given that we are two open and curious characters, this 'hybrid domesticity' is ideal."

Above: In the little study, the red-lacquered book-cases, designed by Stefano Giovannoni, frame a *4 Gopuram* table by Ettore Sottsass for the *Bharata* collection of Design Gallery, Milano.

Opposite: The bedroom is in a corner of the space. The furnishings are spare, consisting of a few items. The bed was designed by Elisa Giovannoni and the dresser is by Johanna Grawunder for Design Gallery, Milano. The star-shaped vase in the window on the left is by Ettore Sottsass, while in the window on the right is an Indian artwork made of papier-mâché.

Overleaf, left: In the foreground, the silver-plated reflective table with decorations dates from the fifties and served as a counter in a jewelry shop in Venice. The chairs are from Emeco.

Overleaf, right: The table is four meters (thirteen feet) long, and it is illuminated by two large *Pudding* hanging lamps from FontanaArte's *Candle* collection. The steel kitchen furniture was designed by Elisa Giovannoni. The kitchen space extends to the exterior, onto the green space of the patio. The flooring, like that on the patio, is teak.

Opposite: The kitchen, seen from the patio where a pomegranate tree and an olive tree grow.
Above: The large terrace on roof has been turned into a genuine hanging garden, subdivided into various zones. The sofas and armchairs on the left were designed by Paola Lenti. The flooring and the custom-made picnic tables and benches on the right are all in teak. Beneath the pergola are several *Air Chairs* by Jasper Morrison for Magis.

Overleaf, left: Various images of the building and the spaces adjoining the pool. From top to bottom: an exterior view of the former industrial building, from the forties, made of red brick; the corner tower, which originally contained a water cistern and is now used as a residential space on various levels; a special kitchen for preparing fish opens out onto the terrace. The large open room, ten meters (thirty-five feet) high, is used as a location for events and occupies the entire ground floor. A stairway leads down to the basement, which has a small spa with a pool and a sauna.
Overleaf, right: The pool in the basement, which is lit by a skylight set in the floor of the large events room on the ground floor, is lined with white Bisazza mosaic tile.

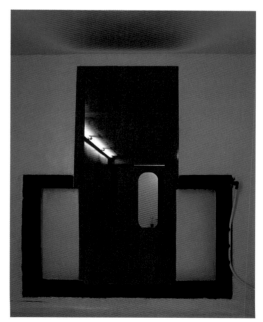

Acknowledgments

We would like to offer our gratitude to all the
designers who gave us their time and opened their
homes and studios. We are also grateful to those
who, for editorial reasons, could not be included in
this volume.

Long conversations with the designers enabled
us to gather not only their stories and anecdotes but
also allowed us to see their way of life and understand their philosophy of design.

Thanks to all those who helped organize the
meetings and photo shoots: Beatrice Felis, Paolo
Imperatori, Angela Ciaccio, Elena Marco, Daniela
Spiezio, Carla Rabuffetti, Monica Del Torchio, Mara
Corradi, Alessandro Marelli, Paola Colombo, Anna
Casati, Giusi Flor, Giulia Reghellin, Tomaso Schiaffino,
Catharin Noorda, Eleonora De Luca, Anna Marin.
Special thanks to Pietro Poli and Steve Sears for
their editorial assistance and to Giorgio Piseri and
all those who offered support during the research
for this book.